PEER GYNT

THE PLAYS OF HENRIK IBSEN
(1828–1906)

WITH THEIR DATES OF COMPOSITION

Catiline (1849)
The Warrior's Barrow (1849–50)
Norma (1851)
St. John's Eve (1852)
Lady Inger of Oestraat (1854)
The Feast at Solhaug (1855)
Olaf Liljekrans (1856)
The Vikings at Helgeland (1857)
Love's Comedy (1862)
The Pretenders (1863)
Brand (1865)
Peer Gynt (1867)
The League of Youth (1868–69)
Emperor and Galilean (1864–73)
The Pillars of Society (1875–77)
A Doll's House (1879)
Ghosts (1881)
An Enemy of the People (1882)
The Wild Duck (1884)
Rosmersholm (1886)
The Lady from the Sea (1888)
Hedda Gabler (1890)
The Master Builder (1892)
Little Eyolf (1894)
John Gabriel Borkman (1896)
When We Dead Awaken (1899)

HENRIK IBSEN, the most influential dramatist since Shakespeare, was born at Skien, Norway, in 1828. After years of failure and poverty, he emigrated at the age of thirty-six to Italy, and there wrote *Brand*, which brought him immediate fame. He remained in self-imposed exile for twenty-seven years, living in Rome, Dresden, and Munich. In 1891 he returned to Norway, and spent the last fifteen years of his life in Christiania (now Oslo). He died there in 1906 at the age of seventy-eight. Ibsen wrote twenty-six plays, sixteen of which are still performed in England and America.

MICHAEL MEYER, the translator, was born in London in 1921. After studying at Oxford he was for three years lecturer in English Literature at Upsala University in Sweden and now lives partly in Stockholm and partly in London. Author of one novel, two plays, and one television play, he is best known as a translator from the Scandinavian languages and has established a unique reputation for himself in this field in England. The first three volumes of his Ibsen translations are *Brand* (Anchor 215), *When We Dead Awaken and Three Other Plays* (Anchor 215b) and *Hedda Gabler and Three Other Plays* (Anchor 215c).

PEER GYNT

BY

HENRIK IBSEN

NEWLY TRANSLATED FROM
THE NORWEGIAN BY
MICHAEL MEYER

Anchor Books
Doubleday & Company, Inc.
Garden City, New York

Anchor Books edition: 1963

CONTENTS

INTRODUCTION   xi

NOTE ON THE TRANSLATION   xxix

Peer Gynt   xxxi

NOTES   159

ACKNOWLEDGMENTS   165

INTRODUCTION

Ibsen wrote *Peer Gynt* in 1867 at the age of thirty-nine,
partly in Rome, partly on the island of Ischia, and partly
in Sorrento. Three years earlier, embittered by poverty
and failure, he had left Norway to settle in Italy; but in
the spring of 1866, the publication of *Brand* had at last
brought him fame and financial security. A short while
previously he had been voted the worst-clothed member
of the Scandinavian community in Rome; now he began
to dress with a touch of dandiness, sporting among other
luxuries a velvet jacket. A new tone appears in his letters;
suspicion and resentment are replaced by a buoyant con-
fidence. Even his handwriting acquired a new assurance.
For the first time in his life, he felt economically secure;
more important, perhaps, he felt that his reputation was
established. This mood was enhanced by the news, in
May 1866, that the Norwegian Government had granted
him an annual pension of 400 specie-dollars; to which
was added 100 specie-dollars from the Philosophical Society of Trondhejm, plus, later in the summer, a further
grant of 350 specie-dollars from a scholarship travel fund.
"I have such a longing for work, such strength," he wrote
to Michael Birkeland on May 4, 1866, "that I could kill
bears!" That autumn he actually asked his publisher,
Frederik Hegel of Gyldendals, not to send him certain
royalties before the following summer, since he did not
want to have a superfluity of cash in Italy.

For a while, however, he remained uncertain in which
direction to apply his energies. Shortly after completing
Brand he had struggled for some weeks with a historical
drama about Magnus Heinesson which he had planned
before leaving Norway. But this came to nothing, and on

May 21, 1866, he wrote to his publisher, Hegel, that he felt more inclined to settle down to the actual writing of *Emperor and Galilean*, the play about the Roman Emperor Julian the Apostate on which he had been researching for two years. On July 22, he wrote to Paul Botten-Hansen: "Now I shall soon start to write in earnest; I am still wrestling with the material, but soon, I know, I shall have the beast under me, and then the rest will glide forward of its own volition." But *Emperor and Galilean* still resisted him, and towards the end of August he laid it aside and set to work revising *Love's Comedy* for a new, Danish edition, removing some of the specifically Norwegian words so as to make the play more palatable to Danish readers. It is possible to discern in this deliberate deletion of Norwegian words the resentment which Ibsen still felt towards his native country, and his contempt for the campaign to purge the Norwegian language of its foreign influences—a campaign which he was shortly to castigate in a more direct and vehement fashion.

Once this work on *Love's Comedy* was finished, Ibsen thought of travelling to Greece (presumably to furnish himself with more material for *Emperor and Galilean*, which partly takes place there), and also to Paris; but both these projects fell through, and he never, to the end of his life, visited either Greece or France. On November 2, 1866, he wrote to Hegel that he was still uncertain to which of several subjects he would next turn: "this very division of interest is proof that none of these themes has as yet sufficiently matured in my mind; but I feel confident that this will soon happen, and hope to be able to let you have the completed manuscript during the spring."

It was around Christmas 1866, or the New Year of 1867, that his plans for *Peer Gynt* began to clarify. On January 5, 1867, he wrote to Hegel: "At last I am able to tell you that my new work is well under way and will, if nothing untoward happens, be ready early in the summer. It will be a long dramatic poem, having as its principal character a part-legendary, part-fictional character from

Norwegian folk lore during *recent* times. It will bear no resemblance to *Brand,* and will contain no direct polemics nor anything of that kind. I have long been pondering the material for this; now the whole plan is worked out and on paper, and I have begun the first act. It grows as I work on it, and I am confident that you will be satisfied with the result."

In point of fact, the dates inscribed by him on his manuscript show that Ibsen did not begin writing the play until nine days after this letter, on January 14, 1867; he had a tendency, not unique among authors, to tell white lies to his publisher. He completed Act 1 six weeks later, on February 25. Six days later, on March 3, he started on Act 2, which, if we are to believe a further letter to Hegel (March 27, 1867) he finished in three weeks. In mid-May he moved from the heat of Rome to the island of Ischia, where he lived for three months in the little town of Casamicciola on the northern side of the island, near the extinct volcano of Epomeo. The weather was exceptionally hot, even for the natives, but Ibsen seemed to revel in it and worked throughout the day; according to Vilhelm Bergsoe, who was with him at this time, he took no siesta but spent the afternoons correcting what he had written in the mornings. He completed Act 3 in as little as two and a half weeks, on July 2. During this month the sirocco arrived and raised the temperature to above 100°, but Ibsen continued to work both afternoon and evening, revising and fair-copying. On August 8 he was able to write to Hegel, still from Ischia:

"I have today sent you, via Consul-General Danchertsen in Naples, the manuscript of the first three acts of my new work, entitled *Peer Gynt,* a dramatic poem. This section will come to around 120 printed pages, and the remainder will add up to about the same. I hope to be able to send you Act 4 towards the end of the month, and the rest not long after that. In case it should interest you, Peer Gynt was a real person who lived in Gudsbrandsdal, probably around the end of the last century or the beginning of this. His name is still famous among the people up there, but not much more is known about his life than what is to be found in Asbjoernsen's *Norwegian Fairy Tales* (in the section entitled *Stories from the Mountains*). So I haven't had much on which to base my poem, but that has meant that I have had all the more freedom with which to work on it."

One night in mid-August there was a slight earthquake on Ischia, and although the natives treated it lightly Ibsen left the island the next day and settled in Sorrento. Here he remained for two months, writing the last two acts; there was no earthquake to trouble him, but in nearby Naples there was an outbreak of cholera, and at one time he thought his wife had caught it; but this fear proved to be unfounded.

We do not know when he began Act 4, but he completed it on September 15, and posted the fair copy to Hegel three days later, adding: "If the printing of the list of characters could be delayed until I have sent you the remainder of the play, I should be grateful, since I might possibly wish to add a few minor characters; but this isn't important." The next day, September 19, he began the final act, and completed it in twenty-five days on October 14. Four days later he posted the fair copy of this to Hegel: "and may luck attend it!"

*   *   *

Hegel was very quick to publish *Peer Gynt* after the success that had attended *Brand*, and it reached the Scandinavian bookshops on November 14, 1867, less than four weeks after he had received the final section of the manuscript. Ibsen was delighted at the book appearing in time to catch the Christmas sales. "Let us hope the critics will be kind to us," he wrote to Hegel on November 23. "I think the book will be much read in Norway."

Peer Gynt, however, gained a mixed reception in Scandinavia. The first omens were good; Hegel sent word that the large first edition had sold out almost at once, and that a second edition of 2000 copies was in the press.

Bjoernson, that most patriotic of poets, who more than most might have been expected to take offence at the fun poked at Norwegian nationalism, wrote Ibsen a letter full of admiration: "I love your spleen, I love the courage with which it has armed you. I love your strength, I love your recklessness—oh, it turned all my thoughts to laughter, like the smell of the sea after the closed air of a sickroom." He also published a review in *Norsk Folkeblad* shortly after the book appeared, praising it hugely.

Ibsen penned a letter of thanks, but before he had posted it he read an attack on the play by Clemens Petersen in the Danish magazine *Faedrelandet*. This was the leading intellectual paper in Scandinavia, having a wide circulation in Norway and Sweden as well as in Denmark, and Petersen had a considerable reputation as a literary pundit; he had written generously, though not uncritically, of *Brand*, and Ibsen had sent him a rather fulsome letter while he was preparing *Peer Gynt*, expressing the hope that Petersen would recognize that in his new work he had "taken a marked step forward." Petersen had some good things to say of *Peer Gynt*, but complained of "a lack of clarity in the conception and of absolute integrity in the execution"; he also declared, somewhat obscurely, that neither *Brand* nor *Peer Gynt* was real poetry because they "lacked idealism," objected that the characters in *Peer Gynt* were not fully rounded or alive, and summed the play up as "an unsuccessful allegory" which frequently degenerated into "an intellectual swindle."

This review so enraged Ibsen that he tore up the letter he had written to Bjoernson and composed another. This second letter reveals an emotional, even hysterical side to Ibsen's character such as he rarely allowed to emerge in his letters or conversation. "Dear Bjoernson," he wrote on December 9, 1867, "What is this curse that at every juncture interposes itself between us? It is as though the Devil came in person to cast his shadow over us . . . An hour ago, I read Hr. Clemens Petersen's review in *Faedrelandet* . . . If I were in Copenhagen and anyone stood as near to me as Clemens Petersen does to you, I would have

struck him senseless before allowing him to commit so
calculated an offence against Truth and Justice . . . My
book *is* poetry; and if it isn't, it will *become* such. The
conception of poetry in our country, in Norway, shall
shape itself according to this book . . . He says that the
Strange Passenger represents the idea of *Angst.* Were I
standing on the gallows and able to save myself by con-
fessing to such an interpretation, the thought would never
have occurred to me; I never dreamed of any such thing;
I merely slipped the scene in as a caprice. And is not Peer
Gynt a character rounded and individual? And the
Mother? . . . However, I am glad that this injustice has
been flung at me; it is a sign of divine aid and dispensa-
tion; anger increases my strength. If there is to be war,
then let there be war! If I am not a poet, what have I to
lose? I shall try my hand as a photographer. I shall deal
with my contemporaries up there, each and all of them,
one by one, as I have dealt with these language reformers;
I shall not spare the child in its mother's womb, nor any
thought nor feeling that may have motivated the actions
of any man who shall merit the honour of being my vic-
tim . . . Do you know that all my life I have turned my
back on my parents, on my whole family, because I could
not bear to continue a relationship based on imperfect understanding?"

He did not post the letter at once, but added a postscript the following day: "I have slept on these words and
read them through in cold blood. The mood they express
is that of yesterday; I shall send them, nevertheless." After
another and equally hysterical outburst ("Do not under-
rate my friends and supporters in Norway; the party whose
paper has allowed its pages to carry an injustice against
me shall realize that I do not stand alone . . . My enemies
shall learn that if I cannot build I have at least strength
enough to destroy") he ended on a scarcely appeasing
note: "I reproach you merely with inactivity. It was not
good of you to permit, by doing nothing, such an attempt
to be made in my absence to put my literary reputation
under the auctioneer's hammer."

Bjoernson accepted this abuse calmly, and wrote Ibsen a letter of splendid generosity and exhortation, begging him to "be just towards us and have faith in yourself." This reached Ibsen on Christmas Day, and so mollified him that in his next letter, on December 28, he actually asked Bjoernson to give Petersen[1] his regards. But his old feeling of resentment soon returned, and it was to be ten years before he wrote to Bjoernson again.

Another Dane to find fault with *Peer Gynt*, and one whose condemnation must particularly have saddened Ibsen, was his old friend and admirer Georg Brandes. Writing in *Dagbladet*, he admitted that it contained great beauties and certain noble truths, but concluded: "Beauties and Truths are far less important than Beauty and Truth in the singular, and Ibsen's poem is neither beautiful nor true; the misanthropy and self-hatred on which it is based are a poor foundation on which to build a work of art . . . What wormwood-tainted joy can he find in thus belittling human nature? It is time this campaign came to an end. We have had enough and the thing must stop." Hans Andersen, too, disliked the play. "Ibsen is repellent to him," wrote Edvard Grieg to Bjoernson, "and *Peer Gynt* the worst that he has read."

In Norway the book was better received than in Denmark, though there, too, the reception was mixed. *Morgenbladet* and *Aftenbladet* published long reviews which were on the whole laudatory; but the greatness of the play was not generally appreciated, at any rate by the critics. Apart from the anti-Norwegianism, some people were bothered by the ending, which they thought facile, and others by what seemed to them an incongruity between the young, the middle-aged and the elderly Peer. Camilla Collett, the pioneer of women's independence in Norway,

---

[1] Petersen suffered swift retribution. Barely a year later, he became involved in a scandal in a girls' school in which he had been lecturing, and was forced to leave for the United States, where he devoted himself to religious journalism among the Scandinavian-Americans—a dreadfully Ibsenish fate to befall a leading literary critic.

was offended by the passivity of Solveig's character, declaring that a more forceful female would have shown Peer the error of his ways much earlier. And Kristofer Janson, the poet, denounced the attack on the language reformers, of whom he was one. Ibsen, who had a long memory, used him seventeen years later as part-model for the self-pitying Hjalmar Ekdal in *The Wild Duck*.

After his first outburst of fury, Ibsen accepted these criticisms calmly. "How goes it with *Peer Gynt?*" he wrote to Hegel on February 24, 1868. "In Sweden, as far as I can tell from the newspaper reviews, it has been very well received; but has it sold accordingly? In Norway I gather the book has caused a great rumpus; which bothers me not in the least; but both there and in Denmark, people have discovered much more satire than I intended. Why can't people read the thing as a poem? That was what I wrote it as. The satirical sections are pretty isolated. But if, as seems to be the case, the Modern Norwegian recognizes himself in Peer Gynt, that is those good gentlemen's own funeral."

*   *   *

Ibsen had no thought, when he was writing *Peer Gynt*, that it should ever be staged; he had too great a contempt for the limitations of the Norwegian theatre and of the men in charge of it. He wrote it, as he had written *Brand*, merely to be read. A short while afterwards, however, the directorship of the Christiania Theatre passed into the hands of an enlightened Swede named Ludwig Josephson. In 1873 Josephson staged both *The Pretenders* and *Love's Comedy* in an imaginative fashion, and it occurred to Ibsen that, if suitably adapted, *Peer Gynt* might receive at the same hands a not unworthy presentation. Before approaching Josephson, however, Ibsen wrote (January 23, 1874) to Edvard Grieg to ask if the latter would consider providing a musical accompaniment and to inform him of his plans regarding suitable cuts, which are sometimes surprising. "Act 1 will be retained in its entirety," he wrote, "apart from some thinning out of the dialogue . . . The wedding scene on p. 28 can be made much more of, with the help of ballet, than appears in the text . . . In Act 2, the incident with the three peasant girls on pp. 57–60 should receive whatever musical treatment you feel appropriate; but there must be devilry in it! . . . There will have to be some kind of musical accompaniment to the scene in the troll palace, though here too the dialogue will be considerably thinned out. The scene with the Boyg, also, which will remain uncut, must have music; the Bird Voices to be sung; the church bells and psalm singing to be heard in the distance . . . Pretty well the whole of Act 4 will be omitted in performance. In its place, I thought we might have a great musical tone-picture to suggest Peer Gynt's wanderings in the wide world, with American, English and French melodies interwoven as changing and disappearing *motifs* . . . Act 5 must be shortened considerably . . . The scenes on the upturned boat and in the churchyard will have to go . . . The scenes with the Button Moulder and the Old Man of the Mountains will be trimmed down. On p. 254 the churchgoers sing on the forest path; church bells and distant psalm singing should be indicated in the music during the dialogue which follows until Solveig's song concludes the play, at which point the curtain will descend while the psalm singing is heard again clearer and louder. This is roughly how I have imagined it . . . If you agree to come in with me on this, I shall immediately approach the management of the Christiania Theatre, send them an acting script and ensure that the play is guaranteed a production. As a fee, I propose to ask 400 specie-dollars, to be shared equally between the two of us."

Grieg did not receive this invitation with unmixed delight. "I can't but admire," he wrote to Bjoernson (September 12, 1874) "the way from start to finish it splutters with wit and venom. But it will never win my sympathy. Though I think it the best thing Ibsen has written. Am I not right? But you don't imagine I had a free choice in the matter! I received the offer from Ibsen last year, and naturally baulked at the prospect of putting music to this

most unmusical of subjects. But I thought of the 200
[specie-dollars] and of the voyage, and made the sacrifice.
The whole thing sits on me like a nightmare." The previ-
ous month, he had written to his friend Frants Beyer:
"It is a dreadfully intractable subject, certain passages ex-
cepted—e.g., the part where Solveig sings—I've done that
all right. And I've made something of the Old Man's palace in the mountains, which I literally can't bear to. listen
to, it stinks so of cow-dung and Norwegian insularity and
self-sufficiency! But I think people will sense the irony
behind it; especially where Peer says: 'Both the dance and
the music were really splendid. May the cat claw me if I
lie!' "

Ludwig Josephson reacted enthusiastically to Ibsen's
proposal, though he begged him not to omit the whole of
Act 4, suggesting instead certain cuts to which Ibsen
agreed. Grieg continued to grouse privately about his
"nightmare," and it was not until eighteen months after
he had accepted the commission, in August 1875, that he
finished the music.

Peer Gynt received its first performance at the Christiania Theatre on February 24, 1876. It was the most expensive production that had yet been attempted in Norway, and was a great success; it was performed thirty-seven
times, and would have continued even longer had a fire
not cut short the run. Despite the cuts, the play lasted
for four and three-quarter hours (from 7 to 11.45 P.M.),
and seems to have been produced with the accent on the
lyrical rather than the satirical aspects. Ibsen did not attend the production, being still reluctant to revisit Norway; but, writing to Josephson from Munich on March 5,
1876, he declared: "The outcome of this bold enterprise
on the part of your theatre has exceeded all my expec-
tations."

Ibsen was still, at this time, little known outside Scandinavia, and it was not until 1880, thirteen years after
the play had been published, that he received a request,
from Germany, for permission to translate it. He replied
to the enquirer, Ludwig Passarge (May 19, 1880): "It

was a surprise to me to learn that you regard this work as suitable to be translated into German for publication there. I must confess that I at least entertain grave doubts on this score. Of all my books I regard *Peer Gynt* as the least likely to be understood outside Scandinavia. I beg you to reflect that few of your German readers will share your own capacity for understanding the poem. You yourself doubtless possess a close knowledge of the Norwegian character and the way the people live; you are acquainted with our literature and our way of speech; you know the people and the personalities one finds up there. But is not all this necessary if one is to find any real flavour in the poem? . . . I hope you will not misconstrue my voicing thus openly the considerations which would, to my mind, operate against your project. I felt it my duty not to conceal them; should they prove unfounded, I shall of course be most gratified."

Ibsen's doubts did indeed prove unfounded, for *Peer Gynt* has become the best known of all his works outside, as inside, Scandinavia. So far from being regarded as exclusively Norwegian, Peer himself seems to have been accepted everywhere as a national prototype; a Japanese critic has described him as "typically Japanese." Subsequent to its premiere in Christiania, *Peer Gynt* was staged before the end of the century in Copenhagen (1886), Gothenburg (1892), Stockholm (1895) and Paris (1896). This last production was by Lugné-Poe, and was the subject of a perceptive notice by Bernard Shaw in the *Saturday Review.* "Ibsen's grip of humanity," he wrote, "is so powerful that almost any presentable performer can count on a degree of illusion in his parts which Duse herself failed to produce when she tried Shakespeare . . . The universality of Ibsen makes his plays come home to all nations, and Peer Gynt is as good a Frenchman as a Norwegian, just as Dr. Stockmann is as intelligible in Bermondsey or Bournemouth as he is in his native town."

The first performance of the play in England[2] took

[2] But there had been an amateur performance in Scotland in 1908.

place on February 26, 1911 at the Rehearsal Theatre in
London with, improbably, an actress, Pax Robertson, in
the part of Peer. (Her mother, Catherine Lewis, ran the
Ibsen Studio, which presented the production.) Among
the many notable interpretations of the role in this century
have been those of Werner Krauss in Berlin and L. M.
Leonidov in Moscow, both in 1928, Gösta Ekman in
Stockholm in 1934, Ralph Richardson in London in 1944
(with Laurence Olivier as the Button Moulder), and Max
von Sydow in Malmö in 1957 (in a production by Ingmar
Bergman). *Peer Gynt* has also been filmed on no less than
three occasions; in America in 1915 (directed by Oscar C.
Apfel, with Cyril Maude); in Germany in 1934 (directed
by Fritz Wendhausen, with Hans Albers); and again in
America in 1941 (directed by David Bradley, with Charl-
ton Heston).

* * *

Apart from what Ibsen had read in Asbjoernsen's col-
lection of fairy tales, the historical-legendary Peer Gynt
of Gudsbrandsdal may well have come to his notice
five years before he wrote the play, when, having been
refused a poet's stipend, he received a kind of consolatory
grant to travel around the Norwegian countryside collect-
ing folk lore. Some doubt exists as to who exactly was the
original of the legend; possibly a Peder Olsen Hage who
died in 1785, possibly one Peder Laurissen who lived a
century earlier. William Archer noted the debts Ibsen's
play owes to Asbjoernsen: the adventure of Gudbrand
Glesne on the Gjendin Edge, the encounter with the three
peasant girls, the meeting with the Boyg, the devil in the
nutshell, the Greenclad One and the Ugly Brat, the proposed correction of Peer's eyesight to measure up to troll
standard, Soria-Moria Castle, and the threadballs (though
these last recur frequently in Norwegian folk lore). The
character of Peer as conceived by Ibsen, however, has
little in common with that of the legendary Peer, and for
this Ibsen seems to have drawn on certain of his contemporaries, including himself. Georg Brandes speaks of
"a young Dane whom Ibsen often saw on Ischia, a notably

affected and pompous daydreamer and braggart. He told the young girls on Ischia and Capri that his father (a schoolmaster) was a close friend of the King of Denmark, and that he himself was a person of great distinction, who sometimes wore a suit of white satin. He called himself a poet, but had to visit wild regions in order to find inspiration . . . He died not far from Ibsen in Rome. Some traits of his character have survived in Peer Gynt." Ibsen's old chief at Bergen, Ole Bull, is also believed to have served as part-model for Peer; soon after he had established his Norwegian Theatre there, he left it (in the spring of 1852) to go to America and found an ideal community on the model approved by the French Socialists. This was to be called Oleana, and Ibsen doubtless had this in mind when he made Peer dream of his ideal community, Gyntiana, in Act 4.

Another who lent something to Peer's character was the poet A. O. Vinje, whom Ibsen had known in his Christiania days, an incurable optimist who was always quoting his own verses and aphorisms. Vinje had written a sequence of attacks on *Brand*, and Ibsen's friends in Norway at once assumed him to have been the model for Peer. And there were several lively young Scandinavian poets in Rome during 1866–1867 who may have contributed something.

Ibsen also confessed, in a letter to Peter Hansen (October 28, 1870) that he had, when creating Peer, drawn on certain traits of his own character. "After *Brand*," he wrote, "*Peer Gynt* followed, as it were, of its own volition. I wrote it in Southern Italy, on Ischia and in Sorrento. Thus far removed from one's readers, one loses one's inhibitions. This poem contains much that has its roots in my own childhood; my mother, with necessary exaggerations, served as the model for Aase." Later he told Georg Brandes that he had used his contrasting memories of life in Skien before his father's bankruptcy and in Venstorp afterwards as "a kind of model for my picture of life in 'the house of rich John Gynt.'"

*   *   *

Peer Gynt is unusual among Ibsen's plays in betraying an apparent debt to certain literary influences. Ibsen owed less to other authors than almost any other writer of comparable stature; he was an unwilling reader, at any rate of books (though he read newspapers most minutely, including the advertisements). Four works, however, all of them Danish, would seem to have left their mark on *Peer Gynt*. One was Frederik Paludan-Müller's epic poem *Adam Homo*, published some twenty years previously, which had already had its effect upon *Brand*. Adam, like Peer, is a weak character who deserts his true love, loses his grip on life, gains riches and worldly success at the cost of his soul, and finally, in the presence of death, senses the possibility of salvation through the love of the woman he had deserted. Another influence, noted by Brandes, appears to have been Oehlenschläger's *Aladdin*. Aladdin, like Peer, is a dreamer; when contemplating suicide he says, in a phrase which has its echo in the last act of *Peer Gynt*:

> *Receive this wretched, failed experiment*
> *Into your crucible. Melt me down again.*

The phrase *at vaere sig selv*, to be oneself, appears in *Aladdin*; and Aladdin's mother, Morgiane, alternates like Aase between admiration and despair at her son's unpredictability. Aladdin, however, is presented as a heroic character, the apotheosis of the dreamer, where Peer is a *reductio ad absurdum* of the type. Oehlenschläger regarded the life of the imagination as the highest form of existence; Ibsen knew its dangers.

Two other works that need to be studied by anyone interested in the origins of *Peer Gynt* are J. L. Heiberg's poem *A Soul after Death* (1840) and Hans Egede Schack's novel *The Fantasts* (1858). Johan Paulsen, who knew Ibsen intimately, has recorded that these were two of the few books that he ever heard Ibsen praise; and that Ibsen once told a young poet that he ought to read everything that Heiberg had written. In *A Soul after Death*, the soul, like Peer, is condemned, not for great sins, but

for common bourgeois pettiness; it had lived only for material comfort, and had never tried to be itself. And there
are two meetings in Heiberg's poem, one between the Actor and Death, and one between the Soul and Mephi-
stopheles, which carry strong echoes of Peer's encounters
with the Button Moulder and the Thin Person. *The Fantasts*, a remarkable psychological analysis of the danger of
daydreaming, would seem to have exerted a general rather
than a particular influence. It is also perhaps worth noting
that Hans Andersen's story *Elverhoej*, itself an earlier satire on Norwegian nationalism, also contained a character
named The Old Man of the Mountains. A sixth Dane,
Soeren Kierkegaard, is supposed by some to have influenced *Peer Gynt*; but the exact measure of Ibsen's debt
to Kierkegaard, if any such debt existed, must remain in
doubt. Ibsen once stated that he had "read little of
Kierkegaard, and understood less"; but many writers have
been unconsciously influenced by authors whom they only
partly understood.

* * *

Some of Ibsen's rough notes for *Peer Gynt* have survived, plus one draft and the fair copy. The notes were
long assumed to have been lost, but as late as 1932 fragments of them were discovered among papers in the pos-
session of his daughter-in-law, Bergliot Ibsen. The first
"ark" of four pages is unfortunately missing, and the
manuscript begins in the middle of Act 2, where Solveig
asks Aase to tell her more about Peer, and ends in the
middle of Act 4. Since nearly three sides of this last four-
page sheet are left blank, it would seem that Ibsen had
made no further notes before beginning to write his first
draft. Neither the notes nor the draft contain any very
significant differences from the play as we know it. The
state of the draft suggests that it was a first one; some
sections were originally written in prose, others in regular
trochaic and iambic metres which he later worked into a
looser rhythm.

The main differences from the final version occur in the

first two acts. Originally, Peer's father was not a wastrel but a "man of honour" whom "Our Lord cut off in his prime," and Peer was not an only son but had an elder brother, a very different character, who was killed in war. The troll scene as at first conceived contained a good deal of satirical matter which Ibsen later deleted; for example, it opened with the trolls irreverently singing "For Norway, the birthplace of heroes," presenting the anthem as a symbol of chauvinism. And there was a scene in Act 2 on the mountain (after Peer's renunciation of Ingrid) between Peer and Solveig, who are later joined by Aase and Solveig's parents; her father tells Peer that he can marry her if he is prepared to go to prison as a penance for his crime, an offer which Peer refuses. Most interesting from a psychological viewpoint is the fact that as originally conceived the Boyg stands outside Aase's house and prevents Peer from returning home to his mother after he has left the troll palace. The notes for this scene read: "He stands in pitch darkness outside Aase's house and finds his way blocked by the Great Boyg. Fights with the Great Invisible One. He wins his way in. It is empty. Fights his way out again. The Boyg is everywhere. Despair seizes him. Alone, alone! Everyone has abandoned him."

A curious fact about these notes is that they give the lie to Ibsen's account of how he wrote the play, as described in his letter to Peter Hansen and also as reported by William Archer. On Ibsen's death in 1906, Archer wrote an article in the *Monthly Review* entitled *Ibsen as I Knew Him,* in which he stated: "He wrote *Brand* and *Peer Gynt* at very high pressure, amounting to nervous overstrain. He would go on writing verses all the time, even when asleep or half awake. He thought them capital for the moment; but they were the veriest nonsense. Once or twice he was so impressed with their merit that he rose in his nightshirt to write them down; but they were never of the slightest use . . . He began *Peer Gynt* at Ischia and finished it at Sorrento. He set to work on it with no definite plan, foreseeing the end, indeed, but not the intermediate details. For instance, he did not know that Peer was to go to Africa. 'It is much easier,' he said, 'to write a piece like *Brand* or *Peer Gynt*, in which you can bring in a little of everything, than to carry through a severely logical scheme, like that of *John Gabriel Borkman*, for example.'"

In fact, we know from Ibsen's letters and from the dates on his manuscript that he began the play not in Ischia but in Rome, and that he had a detailed synopsis worked out well past the opening of the African sequence.

* * *

Peer Gynt is usually produced on the stage as an amiable and confused pantomime, with many unnecessary scenes and a facilely happy ending. As written it is as disturbing and uncomfortable a play as *Brand*. Mr. Michael Elliott, who directed the Old Vic production for which this translation was commissioned, has said that *Peer Gynt* is about the struggle between man's deeper self, which he is for ever trying to discover and express, and his surface, animal self, his troll self. On the one hand, there is the divine purpose; on the other, our passions and egocentricities. Life, like the play, is a struggle between these two selves. For trolls exist in man as well as in the mountains. Trolldom traps man through his pride, greed and ambition. Peer Gynt is an Emperor *manqué*, searching to discover what he is Emperor of—to find at the end that the one thing of which he was meant to be, and was not, Emperor, was himself. Mr. Elliott believes, and I agree, that the Strange Passenger, like the hawk in *Brand*, is the thing that destroys you because you have rejected and excluded it; and that the turning-point in Peer's quest for salvation is that moment of despair when he sees the star fall, because the moment of despair is the moment of hope.

What are trolls? Professor Francis Bull has written that they "may be said to represent the evil forces in Nature, at first only as incarnations of frightening sounds and visions from without, but in more recent literature gradually taken in a wider sense, embodying or symbolizing those powers of evil, hidden in the soul of man, which may at times suddenly suppress his conscious will and dominate his actions. . . . In . . . *The Master Builder*, which is very much the author's personal confession, Solness, half in joke and half in earnest and remorse, tells about his devils or trolls; in a way they serve him, but by ever pandering to his evil instincts and desires, they have come to be really his rulers—mysterious powers that make him afraid of himself."

Twenty years after he had completed *Peer Gynt*, Ibsen wrote a letter to its first German translator, Ludwig Passarge, in which he seems to endorse this view that the play is about the struggle between the troll in man and the divine purpose. Referring specifically to *Peer Gynt*, he stated (June 16, 1890): "Everything that I have written is most minutely connected with what I have lived through, if not personally experienced; every new work has had for me the object of serving as a process of spiritual liberation and catharsis; for every man shares the responsibility and the guilt of the society to which he belongs. That was why I once inscribed in a copy of one of my books the following dedicatory lines:

> To live is to war with trolls in heart and soul.
> To write is to sit in judgment on oneself."

MICHAEL MEYER

NOTE ON THE TRANSLATION

Peer Gynt is the most difficult of Ibsen's plays to translate, because the style is continually changing. Although
it is written in rhyme throughout, Ibsen employed half a
dozen different measures. In the first three acts, where
Peer is a peasant of twenty, the language resembles nothing so much as that of *The Playboy of the Western
World*, with its ebullience, naivety and extravagant im-
agery. In the fourth act, Peer is a middle-aged man of the
world, and talks in a pretentious, would-be epigrammati-
cal style like a character from one of Mr. Aldous Huxley's
early novels; while the fifth act is—I had almost said Shakespearean, but that is not quite accurate; the conception is
Shakespearean, but the style remains racy and colloquial;
its characteristic quality, as Archer observed, is its ver-
nacular ease and simplicity, so that when one reads the
play in Norwegian one has no feeling of incongruity between the various sections. As with *Brand*, a free verse,
with broken rhythms, seemed the only answer, apart from
certain passages which demand rhyme.

Wherever I have had to choose between maintaining
the rhythm and using the most effective phrase, I have
not hesitated to prefer the latter. As long as each section
is controlled by a general overall rhythm, the individual
phrase or line can, and indeed, I believe, should break out
of it. This translation was originally much more regular;
a good deal of valuable fragmentation took place during
rehearsal.

The text is presented complete and unabridged. Cuts
made for the 1962 Old Vic production are indicated by
square brackets.

M. M.

PEER GYNT

CHARACTERS

AASE, a farmer's widow.

PEER GYNT, her son.

TWO OLD WOMEN, with sacks of corn. ASLAK, a smith.
  WEDDING GUESTS. A MASTER COOK. A FIDDLER, etc.

SOLVEIG'S FATHER and MOTHER, immigrants.

SOLVEIG and HELGA, her sister.

THE FARMER AT HEGGSTAD.

INGRID, his daughter.

THE BRIDEGROOM and his PARENTS.

THREE SAETER GIRLS. A GREENCLAD WOMAN.

THE OLD MAN OF THE MOUNTAINS.

A TROLL COURTIER. SEVERAL OTHERS. TROLL MAIDENS and
  TROLL CHILDREN. TWO WITCHES. IMPS, GOBLINS, GNOMES,
  etc.

AN UGLY CHILD. A VOICE IN THE DARKNESS. BIRD VOICES.

KARI, a cottar's wife.

MASTER COTTON, MONSIEUR BALLON, HERR VON EBERKOPF
  and HERR TRUMPETERSTRAALE, travellers. A THIEF and
  A RECEIVER.

ANITRA, daughter of a Bedouin chieftain.

ARABS, SLAVE WOMEN, DANCING GIRLS, etc.

THE MEMNON STATUE (singing). THE SPHINX AT GIZEH
  (mute).

PROFESSOR BEGRIFFENFELDT, D. Phil., director of the
  asylum in Cairo.

HUHU, a language reformer from the Malabar coast. HUS-
  SEIN, an Oriental Minister. A FELLAH, carrying a royal
  mummy.

SEVERAL MADMEN, with their keepers.

A NORWEGIAN SKIPPER and his CREW. A STRANGE PASSENGER.

A PRIEST. A FUNERAL PROCESSION. A PARISH OFFICER. A
  BUTTON MOULDER. A THIN PERSON.

The action, which opens in the early years of the last century and closes about fifty years later, takes place partly in the Gudbrand Valley in Norway and on the mountains around it, partly on the Moroccan coast, partly in the Sahara Desert, the asylum in Cairo, at sea, etc.

This translation of *Peer Gynt* was commissioned by the Old Vic Theatre Trust, and was first performed at the Old Vic Theatre, London, on September 26, 1962. The cast was:

AASE	Catherine Lacey
PEER GYNT	Leo McKern
TWO OLD WOMEN	Ida Goldapple Brenda McGuinne
ASLAK	Brian Coburn
MASTER COOK	Endré Muller
SOLVEIG'S MOTHER	Phillada Sewell
SOLVEIG'S FATHER	Fulton Mackay
SOLVEIG	Dilys Hamlett
HELGA	June Dartnall
INGRID'S FATHER	Esmond Knight
BRIDEGROOM	Trevor Peacock
BRIDEGROOM'S FATHER	Anthony Moreton
BRIDEGROOM'S MOTHER	Stella Lewis
INGRID	Adrienno Corri
SAETER GIRLS	Irene Hamilton Judi Bloom Anna Middleton
THE GREENCLAD ONE	Adrienne Corri
OLD MAN OF THE MOUNTAINS	Esmond Knight
OLDEST TROLL COURTIER	Russell Hunter
UGLY CHILD	Francis Attard
THE BOYG	Leo McKern
KARI	Ida Goldapple
MR. COTTON	Anthony Moreton

M. BALLON	Vernon Dobtcheff
HERR VON EBERKOPF	Esmond Knight
HERR TRUMPETERSTRAALE	James Maxwell
OVERSEER	Jeffry Wickham
THIEF	Endré Muller
RECEIVER	Patrick Kavanagh
ANITRA	Adrienne Corri
BEGRIFFENFELDT	James Maxwell
HUHU	James Kerry
FELLAH	Fulton Mackay
HUSSEIN	Russell Hunter
SHIP'S CAPTAIN	Eric Thompson
BOATSWAIN	James Kerry
STEERSMAN	Eric Flynn
WATCH	Jeffry Wickham
COOK	Anthony Moreton
STRANGE PASSENGER	Vernon Dobtcheff
PRIEST	Fulton Mackay
PARISH OFFICER	Russell Hunter
BUTTON MOULDER	Wilfrid Lawson
THIN PERSON	David William

Designed by Richard Negri

Produced by Michael Elliott

Also in the cast were Peter Brookes, Roger Clissold, Robert Hewitt, Ian Hughes, Rosalind Knight, Barbara Latham, Fletcher Lightfoot, Barry Usher, Michael Wells, Fiona Walker and Rosalind Whitman.

ACT ONE

A wooded hillside near AASE's farm. A stream is rushing down it. On the far side is an old millhouse. It is a hot summer's day.

PEER GYNT, a strongly built youth of twenty, comes down the path. AASE, his mother, small and frail, follows him. She is angry and is scolding him.

AASE. Peer, you're lying!

PEER (without stopping). I am not!

AASE. Well, then, swear it's true!

PEER. Why swear?

AASE. Ah, you daren't! It's all rubbish.

PEER (stops). It's true, every word.

AASE (squares up in front of him). Aren't you
      ashamed?
   First you sneak off into the mountains
   For weeks on end in the busy season
   To stalk reindeer in the snow—
   Come home with your coat torn,
   Without the gun, without the meat.
   And then you look me straight in the face
   And try to fool me with your hunter's lies!
   Well, where did you meet the buck?

PEER. West near Gjendin.

AASE (laughs scornfully). Did you, now?

PEER. I suddenly smelt him on the wind.
   Hidden behind an elder-bush
   He was scratching in the snow for lichen—

AASE (still scornfully). Oh, yes!

PEER. I held my breath
    And stood listening. I heard his hoof
    Crunch, and saw one branching antler.
    I wormed on my belly through the stones towards him.
    Still hidden, I peered out.
    Oh, mother, you never saw such a buck!
    So sleek and fat—!

AASE. No, I'm sure!

PEER. I fired. Down he dropped, smack on the hill!
    But the moment he fell, I straddled his back,
    Seized his left ear, and was about
    To plunge my knife into his neck—
    Aah! The brute let out a scream,
    Suddenly stood on all fours,
    Hit the knife and sheath from my hand,
    Forced its horns against my thigh,
    Pinned me tight like a pair of tongs,
    And shot right on to the Gjendin Edge!

AASE (*involuntarily*). In the name of Christ!

PEER. Have you seen the Gjendin Edge?
    Three miles long and sharp as a scythe.
    Down over glacier, slide and cliff,
    [Straight down over sheer grey scree],*
    You can see, on either side,
    Straight into the lakes that sleep
    Black and heavy, more than four thousand
    Feet below. The length of the Edge
    He and I cut our way through the air.
    I never rode such a steed!
    Before us as we thundered
    It was as though there glittered suns.
    Brown backs of eagles swam
    In the huge and dizzy void halfway between us
    And the lakes below—they fell behind
    Like motes of dust. Ice-floes broke
    And crashed on the shore, but we couldn't hear their
        thunder.

* Square brackets indicate cuts made for the 1962 Old Vic production.

Only the spirits of dizziness leaped
As in dance. They sang, they swung in a ring
In my eyes and ears.

AASE (*dazed*). Ah, God preserve me!

PEER. Suddenly, on a sheer impossible spot
A great cock-ptarmigan flew into the air
Flapping, cackling, terrified,
From the crevice where it lurked
Hidden at the buck's foot on the Edge.
He swung half round, gave a high leap to heaven,
And down we both plunged into the abyss!
    (AASE *totters and gropes at the trunk of a tree.*
             PEER *continues.*)
Behind us the black walls of the mountain,
Beneath a bottomless void!
First we clove sheets of mist, then a flock of gulls,
Which turned in the air and fled to every side,
Screeching. Still we fell.
But in the abyss something gleamed
Whitish, like a reindeer's belly.
Mother, it was our own reflection
In the calm water of the mountain lake,
Darting up towards the surface
With the same wild speed with which we fell.

AASE (*gasps for breath*). Peer! God help me! Tell me
    quickly—!

PEER. Buck from air and buck from deep
In a moment smashed together,
So that the foam rose high about us.
We plunged, we gasped and choked.
At long last, mother, I don't know how,
We reached the northern shore.
The buck swam, and I hung behind him.
I ran home—

AASE. But the buck, Peer?

PEER. Oh, still there, I expect.
    (*Snaps his fingers, turns on his heel, and adds:*)
If you find him, you can have him.

AASE. And you haven't broken your neck? Or both
Your legs? Not fractured your spine? Oh, Lord,
Praise and thanks be to Thee, who saved my son!
Your breeches are torn, but what's that
When one thinks what you might have suffered in such
      a fall—?
      (*Stops suddenly, stares at him open-mouthed,*
   wide-eyed, and speechless. At length she explodes.)
Oh, you bloody story-teller! How you can lie!
I remember now, I heard all this rubbish
Before, when I was a girl of twenty.
It happened to Gudbrand Glesne, not to you,
You—!

PEER. To both of us.
Such a thing can happen twice.

AASE (*hotly*). Yes, a lie can be stood on its head,
Smartened up and put in new clothes,
So its own mother wouldn't know its skinny carcase.
[That's what you've done, letting on wild and great,
Tricking it out with eagles' backs
And all that humbug, lying right and left,
Yarning away and scaring me dumb
So I couldn't recognize a story
I'd heard in my mother's lap.]

PEER. If anyone else spoke to me like that
I'd bash him senseless.

AASE (*weeps*). Oh God, I wish I was dead.
I wish I was asleep in the black ground.
Prayers and tears don't touch him. Peer, you're lost,
And always will be.

PEER. Dear, beautiful, little mother,
Every word you say is the truth.
Calm yourself. Be happy—

AASE. Shut up!
How can I be happy with such a pig for a son?
Isn't it bitter for a poor, helpless
Widow like me to be always put to shame?
                    (*Weeps again.*)

What has the family left now from the days
When your grandfather was a wealthy man?
Where are the sacks of silver
Left by old Rasmus Gynt? Your father
Gave them feet, wasted them like sand,
Bought land in every parish, drove
In gilded carriages! Where's what he wasted
At the great winter feast, when every guest
Threw glass and bottle over his shoulder
To splinter against the wall?

PEER.　Where are the snows of yesteryear?

AASE.　Shut up while your mother's speaking!
Look at the house!
Half the window-panes stuffed with rags,
Hedge and fence fallen down,
Cows and chickens exposed to wind and weather,
Fields and meadows lying fallow,
Never a month but I have the bailiffs in—

PEER.　Stop that old wives' tattle!
Many's the time our luck has failed—
[And sprung again to its feet as tall as ever.]

AASE.　[There's salt strewn where that grew.] Lord, you're
　　　a fine one!
[As proud and uppish as ever, just as bold
As when the priest that came from Copenhagen,
Asked you your name, and swore it was one
That many a prince where he came from would envy
　　　you,
So that your father gave him a horse and bridle
In gratitude for his civil talk.
Oh, things were fine then. The Bishop and the Captain
And all the rest of them turning up every day,
Guzzling and boozing and stuffing themselves
Till they were nearly bursting. But
It's when times are hard that a man knows his neigh-
　　　bour.
Empty and silent it was here the day
John Moneybags set off to tramp the roads

With a pedlar's pack on his shoulder.
    (*Dries her eyes with her handkerchief.*)
You're a fine, strong lad]. You ought to be a rod
And staff for your frail old mother, work the farm,
And guard the little you've left of your inheritance.
    (*Weeps again.*)
God help me, it's little use I've had of you!
Lounging all day by the hearth, poking the embers,
Frightening the girls out of the barn on dance-nights,
Making me the game of the whole county
And swapping blows with every ruffian in the parish—

PEER (*walks away from her*).   Oh, let me be!

AASE (*follows him*).   Can you deny you were the ring-
    leader
In that shindy at Lunde, when you fought
Like mad dogs. Wasn't it you who broke
The arm of Aslak the smith? Or at least
Put one of his fingers out of joint?

PEER.   Who's been filling your ears with such rubbish?

AASE (*heatedly*).   The crofter's wife heard him hollering.

PEER (*rubs his elbow*).   No, that was me.

AASE.   You?

PEER.   Yes, mother. I was the one that took the beating.

AASE.   What!

PEER.   He's a nimble man.

AASE.   Who's nimble?

PEER.   Aslak the smith. I'm telling you, I know.

AASE.   Shame upon you, shame! Now I must spit!
    That loafing sot, that swaggerer,
    That boozing sponge! Did you let him beat you?
    (*Weeps again.*)
Many's the shame I've suffered, but this is the worst.
Nimble, is he? Need you be weak?

PEER.   Whether I bash a man or get bashed,
    You start moaning. (*Laughs.*) Now cheer up, mother—

AASE.   What! Have you been lying again?

PEER.   Yes, just this once. So dry your tears.
            (*Clenches his left fist.*)
   This was my tongs. With this I held the smith
   Bent double; my right fist was my hammer—

AASE.   Oh, you ruffian! You'll send me to my grave!

PEER.   No, you're worth better. Twenty thousand times
            better.
   Sweet, ugly little mother, you take my word.
   The whole parish shall honour you. Just wait
   Till I do something, something really big!

AASE (*snorts*).   You!

PEER.   Who knows what will happen?

AASE.   You'll learn to mend your breeches first!

PEER (*hotly*).   I'll be King! Emperor!

AASE.   God help me!
   Now he's losing the little wit he's got.

PEER.   Yes, I will! Just give me time!

AASE.   Oh, yes! I've heard that one before.

PEER.   You'll see, mother!

AASE.   Shut your gullet. You're out of your mind.
   Oh, it's true enough something might have come of you
   If you hadn't got lost in lies and twaddle.
   The Heggstad girl fancied you.
   You could have won her easily if you'd wanted—

PEER.   Do you think so?

AASE.   Her dad's a ninny, he'd not have argued with her.
   He's a stubborn old fool, but she gets her way in the
            end,
   And where she leads he'll follow, grumbling.
            (*Begins to weep again.*)
   Ah, Peer, my son, she's rich. The land's all hers.
   Just think. If you'd only put your mind to it
   You'd be wearing the bridegroom's coat,
   Not standing here black and tattered.

PEER (*briskly*).   Come on, let's go a-wooing!

AASE.   Where?

PEER. At Heggstad.

AASE. My poor boy, you'll find no bride there.

PEER. Why?

AASE. [Wait while I dry my eyes.]
You've lost your chance, your luck's ended—

PEER. How?

AASE (*gulps*). While you were away
In the western mountains, riding stags through the air,
Mads Moen's got the girl.

PEER. What! That scarecrow?

AASE. Yes, now she's taking him to her bridal bed.

PEER. Wait here while I harness a horse to the cart—
                    (*Turns to go.*)

AASE. Save your pains. The wedding's tomorrow.

PEER. Good. I'll be there tonight.

AASE. Shame on you! Haven't I grief enough?
[Without your bringing a general scorn on our heads.]

PEER. Don't worry, it'll be all right.
            (*Shouts and laughs at the same time.*)
Yippee, mother! We'll do without the cart.
I can't waste time running after the mare—
                    (*Lifts her high into the air.*)

AASE. Put me down!

PEER. No! I'm carrying you to my wedding in my arms!
            (*Wades out into the stream.*)

AASE. Help! Lord save us! We'll be drowned!

PEER. I was born for a nobler death—

AASE. Yes! You'll end by being hanged!
            (*Seizes him by the hair.*)
Oh, you brute!

PEER. Keep still. The bottom's slippery here.

AASE. Donkey!

PEER. That's right; carry on. [Talk never hurt a man.]
Look, now it's getting shallow again—

AASE. Don't drop me!

PEER. Git up there now, hup! Let's play Peer and the
stag.
>   (*Gallops.*)
You're Peer and I'm the stag.

AASE. I'm out of my wits!

PEER. There, we've made it.
>   (*Wades ashore.*)
Give your stag a nice kiss.
Let the driver have his fare.

AASE (*boxes his ears*). That's your fare!

PEER. Ow! That's a fine reward! Mother!

AASE. Put me down!

PEER. First to the wedding. You must speak for me.
You're clever. Talk to the old fool.
Say Mads Moen's a good-for-nothing—

AASE. Down!

PEER. And tell him what a fine fellow is Peer Gynt.

AASE. Never you fear! A grand character I'll give you!
I'll tell them all about you, I'll tell them
All your devilries—

PEER. Oh?

AASE (*kicks him angrily*). I won't stop
Till the old man sets his dog on you like a tramp.

PEER. Hm. Then I'll have to go alone.

AASE. Yes, but I'll follow.

PEER. Dear mother, you haven't the strength—

AASE. Haven't I? The way I feel
I could crumble rocks in my bare fingers.
Ugh, I could eat flints! Put me down!

PEER. All right, if you promise—

AASE. Promise nothing! I'm coming there with you.
I'll let them know you for what you are.

PEER. You'd better stay here.

AASE. No. I want to go with you.

PEER. Sorry.

AASE. What are you going to do?

PEER. Put you on the millhouse roof.
          (*He puts her up there.* AASE *screams.*)

AASE. Take me down!

PEER. Yes, if you'll listen—

AASE. Don't be a fool—

PEER. Mother dear, I beg you—

AASE (*throws a turf at him*). Peer, take me down this
          instant!

PEER. I would if I dared.
                    (*Comes closer.*)
    Remember, sit still now. Don't kick
    Or start pulling down the tiles, or you'll hurt yourself.
    [And maybe fall down.]

AASE. You brute!

PEER. Don't kick!

[AASE. Oh, why weren't you blown up the chimney like a
          changeling![1]

PEER. Mother, for shame!]

AASE. Grr!

PEER. Give me your blessing on my journey. Will you?
          What?

AASE. I'll thrash you, you hulking lump!

PEER. Well, goodbye then, mother dear.
    Be patient. I shan't be long.
  (*Moves away, but turns and raises his finger warningly.*)
    Remember now. No kicking.
                    (*Goes.*)

AASE. Peer! God help me, he's going! Liar!
    You with your tales of riding on stags!
    Hi! Will you listen to me? No, he's gone.
                    (*Screams.*)
    Help! I'm getting giddy!
              (TWO OLD WOMEN *with sacks of corn on
              their backs come down towards the mill.*)

FIRST OLD WOMAN. God a'mercy, who's that screaming?

AASE. It's me!

SECOND OLD WOMAN. Aase! Look! Well, you've gone up in the world!

AASE. Not far enough. Please God I'll soon be in heaven.

FIRST OLD WOMAN. Have a nice trip.

AASE. Get a ladder! I must get down!
That devil Peer—!

SECOND OLD WOMAN. Is it your son—?

AASE. Now you can say you've seen with your own eyes
What he gets up to.

FIRST OLD WOMAN. We will.

AASE. Help me down! I've got to get to Heggstad—

SECOND OLD WOMAN. Is he there?

FIRST OLD WOMAN. Then you'll be revenged. The blacksmith's coming too.

AASE (*wrings her hands*). Oh, God protect the boy!
They'll kill him before he's through.

FIRST OLD WOMAN. Well, it's happened before.
Comfort yourself. [It's the ways of Providence.]

SECOND OLD WOMAN. She's out of her mind.
(*Shouts up the hill.*) Eyvind! Anders! Come down here!

MAN'S VOICE. What's the matter?

SECOND OLD WOMAN. Peer Gynt's put his mother on the millhouse roof!

A small hill with bushes and heather. The high road crosses behind it, with a fence running alongside. PEER GYNT *comes along the footpath, walks briskly up to the fence, stops, and looks out across the landscape.*

PEER. There lies Heggstad. I'll soon be there.
(*Climbs half over the fence, then stops and thinks.*)
Is Ingrid sitting there alone, I wonder?
(*Shades his eyes and peers.*)

No, the guests are swarming in like mosquitoes.
Hm. Perhaps I'd better turn back.
> (*Swings back his leg.*)

People always snigger behind your back,
And whisper so that it burns right through you.
> (*Walks a few paces from the fence
> and absently plucks a few leaves.*)

If only I had a dram of something strong.
Or could go unnoticed. [If only they didn't know me.]
A drink'd be best. Then the laughter doesn't bite.

(*Suddenly he looks round as though frightened, then
hides among the bushes. Some* GUESTS *carrying gifts of
food for the wedding walk down past him in the direction
of the farm.*)

A MAN (*in conversation*). His dad was a boozer and his
 ma's a ninny.

A WOMAN. It's no wonder the lad's a good-for-nothing.
(*They pass on. A few moments later* PEER GYNT *reappears. He looks after them, his face red with shame.*)

PEER. Were they talking about me?
> (*With a forced toss of the head.*)

Well, let them talk. That won't kill me.
(*Throws himself down in the heather, lies full length
on his back with his hands beneath his head and stares at
the sky.*)

What a strange cloud! It's like a horse.
There's a man on it too, with saddle and bridle.
And behind him's an old woman riding a broomstick.
> (*Chuckles to himself.*)

It's mother.
She's scolding and screaming: "You brute! Stop, Peer!"
> (*Gradually closes his eyes.*)

Yes, now she's afraid. Peer Gynt rides at the head
Of a mighty army. His horse has a crest
Of shining silver and four shoes of gold.
He has gloves on his hands and a sword and a scabbard,
And a trailing cloak lined with scarlet silk.
It's a fine bold body of men he has with him,

But none sits his horse as proudly as he,
Or glitters as he does against the sun.
Crowds throng below as he passes by them.
They take off their hats and their eyes gape up at him.
The women curtsey, for everyone knows
Emperor Peer Gynt and his thousand warriors.
He scatters sovereigns and shining shillings
On the roadside like pebbles. Every man
In the parish he'll make as rich as a lord.
Peer Gynt rides high over the white sea. The Prince
Of England stands on the shore and waits for him.
And all the maidens of England are with him,
The great men of England and the mighty King
Of England himself rise in homage
From their high table as Peer Gynt comes riding.
King raises his crown from his head and says—

ASLAK THE SMITH (*to several others as they walk past on the far side of the fence*). If it isn't that boozing pig Peer Gynt!

PEER (*half-raises himself*). What's that, Your Majesty?

ASLAK (*leans on the fence and grins*). Time to get up, me lad.

PEER. What the devil—?
Is it Aslak the Smith? What the hell do you want?

ASLAK (*to the others*). He's still dopey from our last encounter.

PEER (*jumps up*). Clear off!

ASLAK. Man, where have you been?
Six weeks away! Did the mountain trolls get you?

PEER. I've been doing strange deeds, Aslak smith.

ASLAK (*winks at the others*). Tell us, Peer.

PEER. It's my business.

ASLAK (*after a moment*). You'll be coming to Heggstad?

PEER. No.

ASLAK. They used to say the girl was keen on you.

PEER. Why, you black crow—!

ASLAK (*takes a step back*). Don't get angry, Peer. If In-
    grid's jilted you

There are others. Think! John Gynt's son!

Come with us to the feast. There'll be juicy young
    lambs,

And widows too—

PEER. Go to hell!

ASLAK. You'll find someone who'll have you.

Good night. I'll give your love to the bride!
        (*They go, laughing and whispering.*)

PEER (*looks after them a moment, tosses his head and half
     turns*). Let her marry whom she pleases!

It's nothing to me.
        (*Looks himself up and down.*)

Breeches torn. Tattered and filthy.

If only I had something new to wear—
          (*Stamps his foot.*)

I'd tear the laughter out of them

Like a butcher pulling the guts from a rabbit.
          (*Looks round suddenly.*)

What's that? Who was that sniggering?

I could have sworn—! I suppose it was no-one.

I'll go home to mother.
       (*Starts up the hill again, but stops
        and cocks an ear towards the fence.*)

The dancing's begun!

(*Stares and listens; walks back down the hill, step by
step. His eyes glitter. He rubs his thigh.*)
             What a fine swarm of lasses!

Seven or eight to every man!

Oh, flames, I must go and join in the fun!

But mother's up on the millhouse roof.
        (*His eyes are drawn towards the feast
           again. He jumps and laughs.*)

Hey, how the dancers fly over the grass!

By God, he's a boy on the fiddle! It laughs

And splutters just like a waterfall.

And oh, what a covey of glittering girls!
Yes, flames, I must go and join in the fun!
(*Leaps over the fence and goes down the road.*)

The farm at Heggstad. In the background is the farm-house itself. Many GUESTS. *A dance is in lively progress on the green. The* FIDDLER *is seated on a table. The* MASTER COOK[2] *stands in the doorway.* KITCHEN WOMEN *carrying food and drink go back and forth between the various buildings.* OLDER PEOPLE *sit here and there chatting.*

A WOMAN (*joins a group sitting on some logs*). The bride? Oh yes, she's crying a little,
But that's always the way.

MASTER COOK (*in another group*). Come on, good people, empty your glasses.

A MAN. Thank you. But you never stop filling them.

A LAD (*to the* FIDDLER, *as he runs past clutching a* GIRL *by the hand*). Play up, man! Don't spare the strings!

GIRL. Scrape till it echoes out over the meadows.

OTHER GIRLS (*in a circle around a* LAD *who is dancing*). That's a fine leap!

A GIRL. He's a nimble leg.

THE LAD (*dancing*). It's a high roof here, and the walls are wide!

BRIDEGROOM (*comes snivelling up to his* FATHER, *who is standing talking to two or three others, and pulls his coat*). She won't, father. She's so proud.

FATHER. What won't she?

BRIDEGROOM. She's shut herself in.

FATHER. Well, find the key.

BRIDEGROOM. I don't know where.

FATHER. You dumb halfwit!
(*He turns back to the others. The* BRIDEGROOM *wanders away across the yard.*)

A LAD (*comes from behind the house*). Hey, girls! Now
     things'll be livening up!
  Here comes Peer Gynt!

ASLAK (*who has just joined them*). Who asked him?

MASTER COOK. Nobody. (*Goes towards the house.*)

ASLAK (*to the* GIRLS). If he tries to speak to you, don't
     listen to him.

A GIRL (*to the* OTHERS). No, we'll pretend we never saw
     him.

PEER GYNT (*enters hot and excited, stops in the middle of
     the* CROWD *and claps his hands*). Now, which
     girl's got the nimblest pair of legs?

A GIRL (*as he approaches*). Not me.

ANOTHER (*similarly*). Nor me.

A THIRD GIRL. I'm sure I haven't.

PEER (*to a* FOURTH GIRL). Well, let's have you, if there's
     no-one better.

FOURTH GIRL (*turns away*). Haven't time.

PEER (*to a* FIFTH). You, then.

FIFTH GIRL (*walks away*). I'm going home.

PEER. Tonight? Are you out of your wits?

ASLAK (*after a moment, in a low voice*). Look, Peer.
     She's dancing with somebody's granddad.

PEER (*turns sharply to an* OLDER MAN). Hey, you! Where
     are the free ones?

MAN. Find them for yourself. (*Walks away from him.*)

(PEER GYNT *falls suddenly silent. He glances shyly and
furtively at the group. They all look at him but do not
speak. He approaches other groups. As he reaches them,
they fall silent; as he walks away, they smile and follow
him with their eyes.*)

[PEER (*quietly*). Their glances and smiles are needles
     in my back.
  My nerves grate like a sawblade under the file.]

(*He walks away along the fence.* SOLVEIG, *holding little*
HELGA *by the hand, enters the yard with her* PARENTS.)

A MAN (*to another standing near* PEER GYNT). Look. The
  strangers.

SECOND MAN. The strangers from the west?

FIRST MAN. Yes, from Heydal.

SECOND MAN. Ah, yes.

PEER (*walks in front of the newcomers, points at* SOLVEIG
  and asks her FATHER). May I dance with your
  daughter?

SOLVEIG'S FATHER (*quietly*). You may; but first we must
  go inside and greet
 The people of the house.

MASTER COOK (*to* PEER, *offering him a drink*). Since
  you've come, you might as well have one.

PEER (*keeps his eyes fixed on them as they go*). Thanks,
  I'm going to dance. I'm not thirsty.
    (THE MASTER COOK *leaves him.* PEER
    looks towards the house and laughs.)

PEER. How fair she is!
 I never saw such a girl! She dropped
 Her eyes to her shoes and her white apron,
 And clutched tight to her mother's skirt,
 And carried a psalmbook wrapped in linen.
 I must look at that girl.
    (*Is about to enter the house.*)

A LAD (*comes out of the house with several others*).
  Why, Peer! Are you leaving the dance already?

PEER. No.

LAD. Then you're heading the wrong way.
  (*Takes him by the shoulder to turn him round.*)

PEER. Let me past!

LAD. Are you scared of the smith?

PEER. I scared?

LAD. Yes, have you forgotten what happened at Lunde?
  (*They all laugh and go down to the dancing-green.*)

SOLVEIG (*in the doorway*). Are you the boy that wanted
  to dance?

PEER. Of course I am. Don't you remember me?
               (*Takes her by the hand.*)
   Come along.

SOLVEIG. I mustn't go far, Mother said.

PEER. Mother said! Mother said! Were you born yesterday?

SOLVEIG. You're making fun—!

PEER. Well, you're almost a child. How old are you?

SOLVEIG. I was confirmed by the priest last year.

PEER. Tell me your name, girl, and we'll talk more easily.

SOLVEIG. My name's Solveig. What's yours?

PEER. Peer Gynt.

SOLVEIG (*draws her hand away*). Oh, heaven!

PEER. What is it now?

SOLVEIG. My garter's come loose. I must tie it tighter.
               (*Leaves him.*)

BRIDEGROOM (*tugs at his* MOTHER'S *dress*). Mother, she
   won't—

BRIDEGROOM'S MOTHER. Won't? Won't what?

BRIDEGROOM. Won't, mother.

BRIDEGROOM'S MOTHER. What?

BRIDEGROOM. Unlock the door.

BRIDEGROOM'S FATHER (*quietly, angrily*). Oh, you're only
   fit to feed with the pigs.

BRIDEGROOM'S MOTHER. No, don't scold him. Poor lad,
   he'll be all right.
               (*They walk away.*)

A LAD (*comes with a crowd from the dancing-green*).
   Have a real drink, Peer?

PEER. No.

LAD. Oh, come on, have a drop.

PEER (*scowls at him*). Have you got some?

LAD. Maybe.
        (*Takes out a pocket flask and drinks.*)
   Oh, how it burns! Well?

PEER. Let's have a sniff. (*Drinks.*)

SECOND LAD. Try mine too.

PEER. No.

SECOND LAD. Come on, now, don't be a fool. Drink up, Peer!

PEER. All right. (*Drinks again.*)

A GIRL (*whispers*). Come on, let's go.

PEER. Are you scared of me, lass?

A THIRD LAD. Who isn't scared of *you*?

FOURTH LAD. You showed us at Lunde what you could do.

PEER. I can do better than that, once I really cut loose.

FIRST LAD (*whispers*). Now he's off!

SEVERAL LADS (*form a circle round him*). Tell us, tell us! What can you do?

PEER. Tomorrow.

THE OTHER LADS. No, now, tonight!

A GIRL. Can you do black magic, Peer?

PEER. I can conjure up the Devil!

A MAN. My grandmother could do that before I was born.

PEER. Liar! There's no one else can do what I can.
Once I conjured him into a nut.
It was worm-eaten, you see.

LADS (*laugh*). Sure, it would be.

PEER. He swore and wept—said he'd give me whatever I wanted

ONE OF THE CROWD. But he had to go in?

PEER. Of course! I plugged the hole with a peg.
Oh, you should have heard him spluttering and skippering!

GIRL. Fancy that!

PEER. Just like a bumble-bee!

GIRL. Have you still got him there?

PEER. No, he's gone back to Hell.
It's his fault the smith doesn't like me.

LAD. Really?

PEER. I went to Aslak and asked if he'd smash it for
me.
He swore he would; put it down on his anvil;
But he's a clumsy lout—well, [it isn't surprising,]
He spends all day swinging that sledgehammer—

A VOICE FROM THE CROWD. Did he kill the Devil, now?

PEER. He laid to like a man.
But the Devil shot in a flame through the roof,
Splitting the walls.

SEVERAL. And the smith—?

PEER.   Stood there
With his hands fried black; since when we've not been
friends.

(They all laugh.)

SEVERAL. That's a good yarn.

OTHERS. It's near his best.

PEER. You think I'm making it up?

A MAN. Oh no, you're not!
I've heard most of it from my granddad.

PEER. That's a lie! It happened to me!

MAN. Sure, what hasn't?

PEER *(with a gesture)*. I can ride through the air on
horseback!
There's a lot I can do, I'm telling you!

(They shout with laughter again.)

ONE OF THE CROWD. Peer, ride through the air for us!

SEVERAL. Yes, dear Peer Gynt!

PEER. Oh, there's no need to beg me!
I'll ride over the lot of you like a storm.
The whole parish shall fall at my feet!

AN OLDER MAN. He's out of his mind.

ANOTHER. He's daft.

A THIRD. You swaggering braggart!

A FOURTH. He's a bloody liar!

PEER (*threatens them*). Just you wait! You'll see!

A MAN (*half drunk*). Just you wait. You'll get your
    trousers dusted.

OTHERS. And a tender bottom. And a fine black eye.
    (*The* CROWD *disperses, the older ones in anger, the
        younger ones laughing scornfully.*)

BRIDEGROOM (*in his ear*). Peer, is it true you can ride in
    the air?

PEER (*brusquely*). I can do anything, Mads. I'm a man,
    believe me.

BRIDEGROOM. Then you've the cloak of invisibility, too?

PEER. The hat, you mean? Of course I've got it.
    (*Turns away from him.* SOLVEIG *walks across the yard
        leading* HELGA *by the hand.*)

PEER (*approaches them. His face lights up*). Solveig!
    Ah, it's good you've come!
          (*Takes her by the wrist.*)
  Now I'll swing you fast and free!

SOLVEIG. Let me go.

PEER. Why?

SOLVEIG. You're so wild.

PEER. So is a stag when spring is dawning.
  Come on, girl, don't be stubborn!

SOLVEIG (*pulls away her arm*). I daren't.

PEER. Why?

SOLVEIG. No, you've been drinking.
          (*Goes away with* HELGA.)

PEER. Oh, to stick a sharp knife through them, all of
    them!

BRIDEGROOM (*nudges him with his elbow*). Can't you
    help me to get at the bride?

PEER (*absently*). The bride? Where is she?

BRIDEGROOM. In the storehouse.

PEER. Mm.

BRIDEGROOM. Oh, come on, Peer Gynt. Please try.

PEER. No, you'll have to manage without my help.
(A thought occurs to him. He says quietly but sharply.)
Ingrid in the storehouse!
(Goes across to SOLVEIG.*)*
Have you changed your mind?
(She turns to go. He steps in front of her.)
You're ashamed because I look like a tramp.

SOLVEIG *(quickly).* You don't! It isn't true!

PEER. It is. And I *have* been drinking, too.
But that was to spite you for hurting me.
Come on, then!

SOLVEIG. I daren't now, even if I wanted to.

PEER. Who are you afraid of?

SOLVEIG. Father, mostly.

PEER. Father? Oh, yes. He's one of those quiet ones.
A godly soul, eh? What? Come on, answer!

SOLVEIG. What shall I answer?

PEER. Is your father a bible man?
And you and your mother, too? Will you answer me?

SOLVEIG. Let me go in peace.

PEER. No.
(Softly but sharply and menacingly.)
I can turn myself into a troll!
I'll come to your bedside tonight at midnight.
If you hear something hissing and spitting
Don't think it's the cat. It's me, my dear!
I'll be drawing your blood in a cup,
And your little sister, I'll gobble her up!
For at night I'm a werewolf. I'll bite you
All over your loins and your pretty back.
(Changes his tone suddenly and begs as though in anguish.)
Dance with me, Solveig!

SOLVEIG *(looks darkly at him).* Now you're ugly.
(She goes into the house.)

BRIDEGROOM (*wanders back*). I'll give you a cow, if you'll only help me.

PEER. Come!

(*They go behind the house. As they do so, a large* CROWD *comes from the dancing-green, most of them drunk. Hubbub and confusion.* SOLVEIG, HELGA *and their* PARENTS *appear in the doorway with some of the* OLDER PEOPLE.)

MASTER COOK (*to* ASLAK *the* SMITH, *who is at the head of the* CROWD). Keep the peace now, will you?

ASLAK (*takes off his coat*). No. We'll settle it now.
Someone's nose must be rubbed in the dirt,
Peer Gynt's or mine.

SOME OF THE CROWD. Sure, let them fight.

OTHERS. No, let's have no violence.

ASLAK. It's fists or nothing.
[For we've come to the stage where words are useless.]

SOLVEIG'S FATHER. Control yourself, man.

HELGA. Are they going to beat him, mother?

A LAD. Let's stuff his lies down his throat.

ANOTHER. Kick him out of the feast!

A THIRD. Spit in his eye!

A FOURTH MAN (*to the* SMITH). Are you backing out?

ASLAK (*throws down his jacket*). I'll slaughter the pig!

SOLVEIG'S MOTHER (*to* SOLVEIG). You see what they think of him?

AASE (*enters with a stick in her hand*). Is my son here?
Wait till I get his pants down!
I'll thrash the holy life out of him!

ASLAK (*rolls up his sleeves*). That stick's too puny for a fat lout like him.

SOME OF THE CROWD. The smith'll thrash him.

OTHERS. Butcher him.

ASLAK (*spits on his hands and nods at* AASE). Hang him!

AASE. What! Hang my Peer? Just you try!

I've teeth and claws! Where is he?
>   (*Shouts across the yard.*)
Peer!

BRIDEGROOM (*enters running*). Oh, God have mercy on
>   us all!
Mother and father, come quickly!

BRIDEGROOM'S FATHER. What's the matter?

BRIDEGROOM. Just fancy! Peer Gynt—!

AASE (*screams*). Have they killed him?

BRIDEGROOM. No, Peer Gynt—! Look up there, on the
>   hillside—!

CROWD. He's got the bride!

AASE (*lowers her stick*). Monster!

ASLAK (*as if thunderstruck*). By God, he's climbing like
>   a goat!

BRIDEGROOM (*weeps*). Oh, mother, he's carrying her like
>   a pig!

AASE (*shakes her fist up at him*). May God strike you
>   down—!
>   (*Shrieks in terror.*)
Be careful!

BRIDE'S FATHER (*enters bareheaded and white with rage*).
>   Bride-rape! I'll have his life for this!

AASE. I'll burn in Hell before you do!

ACT TWO

A narrow path high up in the mountains. It is early morning. PEER GYNT *is hurrying ill-temperedly along the path.* INGRID, *still half-dressed in her bridal clothes, is trying to hold him back.*

PEER. Get away from me!

INGRID (*weeps*). After this! Where can I go?

PEER. Anywhere you like.

INGRID (*wrings her hands*). You have betrayed me!

PEER. It's no good moaning. It's finished.

INGRID. Our crime binds us. Our double crime.

PEER. All memories belong to the Devil.
All women belong to the Devil.
Except one—

INGRID. Which one?

PEER. Not you.

INGRID. Who is it, then?

PEER. Go! Go back where you came from!
Quick! To your father!

INGRID. Dear, kind—!

PEER. Oh, shut up.

INGRID. You can't mean what you say.

PEER. Can and do.

INGRID. To seduce me, and then leave me!

PEER. What wealth have you to offer me?

INGRID. Heggstad farm, and more besides.

PEER. Have you a psalmbook wrapped in linen?
Golden hair about your shoulders?

Do you drop your eyes to your apron?
Do you cling to your mother's skirt?
Tell me!

INGRID. No, but—?

PEER. Did you read with the priest last spring?

INGRID. No, but Peer—?

PEER. Is there modesty in your eyes?
When I ask, do you deny?

INGRID. Oh God—I think he's mad—

PEER. When I see you, does the sun shine?
Well!

INGRID. No, but—

PEER. What's all the rest, then? (*Turns to go.*)

INGRID (*steps in front of him*). Don't you know they'll
hang you if you leave me?

PEER. All right!

INGRID. You can have wealth and honour if you take
me—

PEER. Can't afford it.

INGRID (*bursts into tears*). You raped me—!

PEER. You were willing.

INGRID. I was desperate.

PEER. I was mad.

INGRID (*threateningly*). You'll pay dearly!

PEER. The dearest payment would be cheap.

INGRID. Your mind's made up, then?

PEER. Like stone.

INGRID. Very well. We'll see who wins.
                    (*Goes down the path.*)

PEER (*is silent for a moment, then suddenly cries*). All
        memories belong to the Devil!
    All women belong to the Devil!

INGRID (*turns her head and shouts scornfully up at him*).
        Except one!

PEER. Yes. Except one.
          (*They go opposite ways.*)

---

*By a mountain lake. The ground is soft and boggy. A
storm is brewing.* AASE, *in despair, is shouting and searching everywhere.* SOLVEIG *has difficulty in keeping pace
with her.* SOLVEIG'S PARENTS *and* HELGA *follow a short way
behind.*

AASE (*waves her arms and tears her hair*). Everything's
          against me. The world's angry!
The sky, the water and the ugly mountains.
The sky's sending down fogs to drive him crazy,
The cunning water's waiting to rob him of his life,
The mountains are throwing landslides and avalanches,
And the whole parish is shouting for his blood.
Which they shan't have, for I can't live without him.
Oh, the fool, to let the foul fiend tempt him!
                    (*Turns to* SOLVEIG.)
Isn't it beyond belief?
He that did nothing but lie and romance,
That never exercised any limb but his tongue,
That never did an honest day's work in his life—
That—! Oh, should I laugh or cry?
Mind, when times were tough we stuck together,
For my man had a tongue red for drink.
An idler he was with his bragging, wasting our wealth,
While I and my baby sat at home
Trying to forget. What else could we do?
For I was never a one for arguing.
[It's fearful to look into the eyes of Fate,
And there isn't a woman but likes to bury her grief,
And shove her cares out of sight if she can.]
Some take to drink, others to lying,
So we took to romancing of princes and trolls
And all kinds of beasts. And stealing brides
From their white wedding-beds. But who'd have thought

Those daft ideas would have stuck in his head?
              (*Frightened again.*)
Ow, what a screech! It's a goblin, sure,
Or a flibbertigibbet! Peer, Peer!
Up there, on that hillock—!
(*She runs up a little hill, and looks out across the
        lake.* SOLVEIG'S PARENTS *come to her.*)
Not a sign of him!

SOLVEIG'S FATHER (*quietly*). The worse for him.

AASE (*weeps*). Oh, my Peer! My lost lambkin!

SOLVEIG'S FATHER (*nods gently*). Yes, indeed. Lost!

AASE. No, don't speak like that!
He's a good lad. There's nobody like him.

SOLVEIG'S FATHER. Foolish woman!

AASE. Oh, yes, yes. I'm foolish. But the boy's all right.

SOLVEIG'S FATHER (*still quiet-voiced and mild-eyed*). His
      heart is hardened. His soul is lost.

AASE (*fearfully*). No, no! Our Lord is not so hard!

SOLVEIG'S FATHER. Do you think he can sigh away his
      debt of sin?

AASE (*eagerly*). No, but he can ride through the air on a
      stag!

SOLVEIG'S MOTHER. Merciful heaven, are you mad?

SOLVEIG'S FATHER (*to* AASE). What do you mean,
      woman?

AASE. No deed's too big for him. You'll see,
If only he lives long enough—

SOLVEIG'S FATHER. It would be best if you saw him hang
      on the gallows.

AASE (*screams*). Providence and Mercy, spare us all!

SOLVEIG'S FATHER. In the hangman's hands,
Please God, his heart will turn to repentance.

AASE (*dazed*). Oh, you'll soon be talking me out of my
      senses.
We must find him.

SOLVEIG'S FATHER. To save his soul.

AASE. And his body!
If he's sitting in the bog, we must haul him out.
If the trolls have got him, we must ring the church
bells.

SOLVEIG'S FATHER. Hm. There's a sheep track here.

AASE. The Lord will repay you for your help.

SOLVEIG'S FATHER. It's my Christian duty.

AASE. Bah! Then the rest are heathen savages.
There wasn't one who would come with me—

SOLVEIG'S FATHER. They know him too well.

AASE. He was too good for them. (*Wrings her hands.*)
And to think—to think his life's at stake!

SOLVEIG'S FATHER. Here's a man's footprint.

AASE. Then it's here we must search.

SOLVEIG'S FATHER. We'll cover the ground up to our
farm.
(*He and* SOLVEIG'S MOTHER *go ahead.*)

SOLVEIG (*to* AASE). Tell me more.

AASE (*dries her eyes*). About my son?

SOLVEIG. Yes. Everything.

AASE (*smiles and tosses her head*). Everything? You'd
soon be weary!

SOLVEIG. You'd weary quicker of telling than I of
hearing.

———

*Low treeless heights at the foot of the mountain plain,
with peaks visible in the distance. Long shadows fall. It
is late in the day.*

PEER (*runs in at full tilt and stops on the hillside*). The
whole parish is after me in a mob!
They've armed themselves with rifles and sticks.
I can hear Ingrid's father hollering at their head.
The news has spread quickly: Peer Gynt's on the loose!

This is better sport than bashing a smith!
This is life! I feel as strong as a bear!
    (*Punches around and jumps in the air.*)
To smash and overturn! To dam the waterfall!
To strike! To wrench the fir up by the root!
This is life. It hardens and elevates.
To hell with all bloody lies!

THREE SAETER[3] GIRLS (*run across the hills screaming and singing*). Trond of the Valfjeld! Boord and Kaare!
Troll-pack! Will you sleep in our arms?

PEER. Who are you calling?

GIRLS. Trolls! Trolls!

FIRST GIRL. Trond! Come gently!

SECOND GIRL. Boord! Come and rape me!

THIRD GIRL. All the beds in the hut stand empty!

FIRST GIRL. Gently means rape!

SECOND GIRL. And rape means gently!

THIRD GIRL. If there aren't any boys, we'll play with trolls!

PEER. Where are the boys, then?

ALL THREE GIRLS (*howl with laughter*). They can't come!

FIRST GIRL. Mine called me his love and called me his darling.
Now he's married to an old grey widow.

SECOND GIRL. Mine met a gipsy-girl north on the moor.
Now they're tramping the roads together.

THIRD GIRL. Mine got tired of our bastard's crying.
Now his head grins high on a stake.

ALL THREE. Trond of the Valfjeld! Boord and Kaare!
Troll-pack! Come and sleep in our arms!

PEER (*takes a sudden leap into their midst*). I'm a three-headed troll, and a boy for three girls!

GIRLS. Three? Could you, lad?

PEER. Try me and see!

FIRST GIRL. To the hut! To the hut!

SECOND GIRL. We've a barrel of mead!

PEER. Let it flow!

THIRD GIRL. There'll be no bed empty this Saturday night!

SECOND GIRL (*kisses him*). He sputters and sparks like white-hot iron!

THIRD GIRL (*kisses him*). Like a baby's eyes from the black bottom of the lake!

PEER (*dances among them*). The heart is heavy, the head plays wanton.
In the eyes, laughter; in the throat, tears.

THE GIRLS (*make long noses towards the mountain tops, scream and sing*). Trond of the Valfjeld! Boord and Kaare!
Troll-pack! Did you sleep in our arms?
(*They dance away across the mountains with* PEER GYNT *among them.*)

Among the Ronde mountains. Sunset. Snow-peaks glitter around.

PEER (*enters dazed and bleary*). Castle rises on castle!
Hey, what a shining gate!
Stop! Will you stop? It's shrinking
Further and further away!
[The weathercock on the steeple
Is lifting its wings to fly.
It's all getting blue and misty,
And the mountain's shut and barred.
What are these trunks and roots
That grow from the clefts in the ridge?
It's soldiers heron-footed;
Now *they*'re fading away!]
It swims before me like rainbows;
It hurts my eyes and brain.

What's that that chimes in the distance?
This weight pressing my eyes?
Ugh, how it splits my forehead—
This binding, white-hot ring!
Oh, I cannot remember
Who in Hell put that round my brain!
                    (*Sinks down.*)
The flight along Gjendin Edge—
It was all a fake and a lie!
Up the cliff with the bride—
Then drunk for a night and a day.
Hunted by hawks and kites,
Threatened by trolls and the like,
Sporting with crazy wenches—
A bloody lie and a fake!
                    (*Stares for a long time upwards.*)
There sail two brown eagles.
The wild geese fly to the south.
And I must trudge here and stumble
Knee deep in the mire and filth.
                    (*Jumps up.*)
I'll join them! I'll wash myself clean,
Scoured by the sharpest winds!
I shall soar! I'll wash myself pure in
The gleaming christening-font!
I'll fly high over the farmhouse,
I'll ride till my black soul shines,
Far over the salty sea
And high over England's prince!
Yes, you can stare, my pretties.
I haven't come here for you.
It's no use standing and waiting—
Well, I might take a minute or two—!
    What? Where have those eagles got to?
Oh, what the hell do I care?
There soars the crown of a gable.
It's rising up everywhere.
It's growing out of the ruins.
The gate stands open and fair.
    Ah, now I recognise it!

It's my granddad's fine new home!
The rags are gone from the windows.
The tumbledown fence is gone.
The light pours from every window.
They're feasting in the great room.
  Look, now the old Bishop's clinking
His knife on his silver cup.
The Captain has tossed back his bottle,
And broken the looking-glass up.
Let them squander away. What do we care?
Hush, mother! We don't have to stint.
The rich John Gynt gives a banquet.
Hurrah for the tree of Gynt!
But what's all this bustle and hubbub?
What can the shouting be?
The Captain's proposing the son's health!
The Bishop is calling for me!
Go in, Peer Gynt, to your judgment.
The welcoming cheers fill the room.
Peer Gynt, thou wast born to greatness,
And to greatness thou shalt come!
(*Takes a running jump forward, but strikes his nose against a rock, falls and remains lying on the ground.*)

A hillside, with great rustling trees. Stars twinkle through the leaves. Birds sing in the treetops. A GREEN-CLAD WOMAN *is walking on the hillside.* PEER GYNT *follows her, indulging in various amorous antics.*

THE GREENCLAD ONE (*stops and turns*). Is it true?

PEER (*makes a cutting gesture with his finger across his throat*). As true as my name's Peer!
As true as you're a beautiful woman!
Will you have me? I'll be good to you.
You shall neither weave nor spin.
I'll fill you with food till you're ready to burst.
I'll never pull you by the hair—

GREENCLAD ONE. Nor beat me?

PEER. What an idea! We princes don't beat women.

GREENCLAD ONE. Are you a King's son?

PEER. Yes.

GREENCLAD ONE. My father's the King of the Ronde.

PEER. Is he? Well, that makes us two of a kind.

GREENCLAD ONE. My father's palace is inside the mountain.

PEER. My mother's is bigger, believe you me.

GREENCLAD ONE. Do you know my father? His name is King Brose.

PEER. Do you know my mother? Her name's Queen Aase.

GREENCLAD ONE. When my father's angry, the mountains crack.

PEER. They shake when my mother opens her mouth.

GREENCLAD ONE. When my father dances he kicks the stars.

PEER. My mother can ride through rivers in flood.

GREENCLAD ONE. Have you any other clothes besides those rags?

PEER. Oh, you should see me in my Sunday suit!

GREENCLAD ONE. I always wear gold and silks.

PEER. They look to me more like tow and straw.

GREENCLAD ONE. Well, there's one thing you must remember.
That is the way of the mountain people.
Everything there has another meaning.
If you come to my father's house, you may easily think
You're just in an ugly heap of stones.

PEER. Well now, it's exactly the same with us.
Our gold may seem scrap to you.
You may think each crystal window-pane
Is just a fistful of socks and rags.

GREENCLAD ONE. Black seems white and ugly seems fair.

PEER. Great seems little and foul seems clean.

GREENCLAD ONE (*falls on his neck*). O, Peer! I see it!
    We were made for each other!

PEER.   As the leg fits the breeches, the comb fits the hair.

GREENCLAD ONE (*calls across the hill*). Bridal steed!
    Bridal steed!
  Come, my bridal steed!

(*A huge pig canters in with a rope's end round its neck
as a bridle, and an old sack as a saddle.* PEER GYNT *swings
himself astride its back and sets the* GREENCLAD ONE *in
front of him.*)

PEER.   Hup, now! We'll ride in through the Ronde gate!
    Gee-up, gee-up, my beauty!

GREENCLAD ONE (*amorously*). Just now I was feeling so
    sad and lonely.
  Who can tell what life will bring in its course?

PEER (*slaps the pig and rides away*). You can tell a great
    man by the cut of his horse!

———————

The palace hall of THE OLD MAN OF THE MOUNTAINS.
A great gathering of TROLL COURTIERS, ELVES *and* GOBLINS.
THE OLD MAN OF THE MOUNTAINS *is seated on his throne,
sceptred and crowned. His* CHILDREN *and* NEAREST RELA-
TIVES *surround him.* PEER GYNT *stands in front of him.
There is a great hubbub in the hall.*

TROLL COURTIERS. Kill him! Kill him! The Christian
    dog
  Has bewitched the Troll King's fairest daughter!

TROLL CHILD. Can I cut off his fingers?

ANOTHER.   Can I pull out his hair?

A TROLL MAIDEN.   Huh, ha! Let me bite his bottom!

TROLL WITCH (*with a ladle*). Shall I boil him down into
    soup?

ANOTHER WITCH (*with a carving-knife*). Shall we roast
    him on the spit or brown him in the pot?

THE OLD MAN OF THE MOUNTAINS. Calm yourselves, my
      children!
               (*Beckons his* COUNSELLORS *nearer.*)
We can't afford to be grand.
We've been slipping backwards in recent years.
Our position has become precarious,
And we can't look down our noses at offers of help.
Besides, the lad has no obvious defects,
And seems well-built. True, he's only got one head,
But my daughter is no better off in that respect.
Three-headed trolls are going right out of fashion.
Even two heads are rare nowadays,
And they are not what they used to be.
               (*To* PEER GYNT.)
So you want my daughter?

PEER. Your daughter, and your kingdom as her dowry.

OLD MAN. You shall have half my kingdom while I live,
And the other half when, eventually, I die.

PEER. That suits me.

OLD MAN. Ah, but wait, my lad.
There are certain promises you, too, must make.
If you break one of them, the pact is broken,
And you shall not leave this place alive.
First, you must swear you'll never think
Of what lies outside the kingdom of the mountain.
Day you must shun, action, and anything touched by
      light.

PEER. Well, if I'm to be King, that's easy.

OLD MAN. Next—and this will test your wits—
               (*Rises in his seat.*)

OLDEST TROLL COURTIER (*to* PEER). Let's see if you have
      a wisdom tooth
To crack the nut of the Troll King's riddle.

OLD MAN. What is the difference between troll and
      man?

PEER. No, difference, as far as I can see.

Big trolls want to roast you, small trolls want to claw
you.
It's the same with us, if we dared.

OLD MAN. True. We're alike in that, and more.
But morning is morning and night is night,
And there is a difference nevertheless.
I'll tell you what it is.
Out there, under the shining vault of heaven,
Men tell each other: "Man, be thyself!"
But in here, among us trolls, we say:
"Troll, be thyself—*and thyself alone!*"[4]

OLDEST COURTIER (*to* PEER). You fathom it?

PEER. Not entirely.

OLD MAN. "Thyself alone!" Those sharp and fateful words
Must be engraven on your crest, my son.

PEER (*scratches behind his ear*). Yes, but—

OLD MAN. They *must*, if you would be master here!

PEER. Oh, hell. All right. I really can't see—

OLD MAN. Next you must teach yourself to value
Our simple and homely way of life.
(*He beckons. Two* TROLLS *with pigs'-heads and
white nightcaps bring in food and drink.*)
Our cake flows from the cow, our mead from the bull.
Don't ask yourself if it tastes sour or sweet.
The main thing is, and this you mustn't forget,
It's all home-made.

PEER (*pushes the things away*). To hell with your home-
made drink!
I'll never get used to this place.

OLD MAN. The bowl goes with it. It's gold. Who owns
The golden bowl has my daughter's love.

PEER (*thoughtfully*). [It is written: "Thou shalt subdue
thy nature."]
Well, I dare say in time it won't taste too bad.
All right! (*Tastes.*)

OLD MAN. That's a sensible lad. Did you spit?

PEER.   Taste is a question of what you're used to.

OLD MAN.   Next you must throw away
Your Christian clothes. For this you must know
To the greater glory of the mountain kingdom.
Everything here is made within the mountain.
Nothing comes from the valley except
The silken bow at the tip of your tail.

PEER (*angrily*).   I haven't got a tail!

OLD MAN.   Well, then you must have one.
Prime Minister, tie my Sunday tail on him.

PEER.   I'll be damned if you will!
Do you want to make a fool of me?

OLD MAN.   You cannot court
My daughter with a bare backside.

PEER.   Make a man into a beast?

OLD MAN.   My son, you're wrong.
I'm only making you a respectable suitor.
You'll have a flame-yellow bow,
Which we count as the highest honour.

PEER (*thoughtfully*).   Well, [they say: "Man is but a
      speck of dust,"
And I suppose] one must toe the line of fashion.
Tie away!

OLD MAN.   You're a co-operative boy.

OLDEST COURTIER.   Now see how well you can flip and
      twitch it!

PEER (*angrily*).   What, will you force me further yet?
Must I give up my Christian faith?

OLD MAN.   No, you're welcome to keep that.
[Faith is free. We charge no tariff there.
You can tell a troll by his outside.]
As long as we agree on manners and dress
You can go on calling your freakish fancies faith.

PEER.   For all your conditions, you're
A more reasonable chap than one might think.

OLD MAN.   My son, we trolls are better than our reputation.

That's another difference between you and us.
But now we're through with the serious business
So let's delight our eyes and ears.
Music-girl, forth! Let the mountain-harp sound!
Dancing-girl, forth! Tread our palace floor!

(*Music and dance.*)

OLDEST COURTIER. How do you like it?

PEER. Like it? Hm—

OLD MAN. Don't be afraid to speak. What do you see?

PEER. Something horribly ugly.
A cow with a harp and a dancing sow.

TROLL COURTIERS. Eat him!

OLD MAN. Remember, his eyes and ears are human.

TROLL MAIDENS. Oh, tear off his ears! Pull out his eyes!

GREENCLAD ONE (*weeps*). Must we hear and endure such insults
While I and my sister play and dance?

PEER. Oh, is it you? Well, you know,
A joke at a feast isn't meant unkindly.

GREENCLAD ONE. Do you swear to that?

PEER. Both the dance and the music were really splendid.
May the cat claw me if I lie!

OLD MAN. That's a funny thing about human nature.
It hangs on to people a remarkable time.
[If it gets a gash in the fight with us,
It leaves a scar, but that soon heals up.]
My son-in-law was proving as pliant as any.
Willingly he's thrown off his Christian clothes,
Willingly drunk from our cup of mead,
Willingly tied a tail to his backside.
So willing, in short, to do all that we bade him,
That I really began to think the old Adam
Had been hunted out of our gate for good and all.
But now he's suddenly popped up again.
Well, well, my son, we must give you some treatment
To cure this human nature of yours.

PEER. What will you do?

OLD MAN. In your left eye
I'll make a little cut, so that you'll see awry.
But all you see will seem bright and fair.
Then I'll nip out your right window-pane—

PEER. Are you drunk?

OLD MAN (*lays several sharp instruments on the table*).
Here you see the glazier's tools.
We'll blinker you, like a surly bull.
Then you'll see that your bride is beautiful.
And there'll be an end to these illusions
Of dancing sows, and cows playing harps—

PEER. This is madman's talk!

OLDEST COURTIER. The Old Man of the Mountains
speaks!
He is wise. It is you that's mad.

OLD MAN. Think how much pain and worry you'll save
yourself.
Don't forget that sight is the source
Of the bitter and searing lye of tears.

PEER. That's true. It says in the holy book:
"If thine eye offend thee, pluck it out."
Wait! Tell me, when will my sight be healed
So that I can see again as a man?

OLD MAN. Never, my friend.

PEER. Indeed! Well, thanks very much.

OLD MAN. Where are you going?

PEER. On my way.

OLD MAN. No, wait. It's easy to get in here,
But the mountain gate doesn't open outwards.

PEER. Surely you'll not keep me by force?

OLD MAN. Now listen, Prince Peer, and be sensible.
You've a talent for trolldom. Isn't that true?
You're already shaping quite like a troll.
And you do want to become a troll?

PEER. Indeed I do.
[For a bride with a well-lined kingdom thrown in

I'd put up with losing a thing or two.]
But there's a limit to everything.
I've accepted a tail, that's true enough;
But I can remove what your Minister tied on.
I've thrown off my breeks. They were old and patched.
But I can soon button them on again.
[And I can just as quickly slip my moorings
From all your mountain way of life.]
I don't mind swearing a cow's a maiden.
One can always swallow an oath.
But to know one can never free oneself,
Nor be able to die like a Christian soul;
To live like a mountain troll all one's days,
And never go back—that's what you want.
And that is something I'll never agree to.

OLD MAN.   Now you're beginning to make me angry.
I'm not to be trifled with. You pale-faced
Pigmy! Do you know who I am?
First you take liberties with my daughter—

PEER.   That's a lie!

OLD MAN.   You must marry her!

PEER.   You dare to accuse—?

OLD MAN.   What! Can you deny
You desired and lusted after her?

PEER (*snorts*).   Is that all? Who the hell cares about
that?

OLD MAN.   You human beings are always the same.
You're always ready to admit an impulse,
But won't accept the guilt for anything
Unless you've actually done it in the flesh.
So you think that lust doesn't count?
Wait. You'll soon see with your own eyes—

PEER.   You won't catch me with a bait of lies.

GREENCLAD ONE.   My Peer, before the year's end you'll be
a father.

PEER.   Open the door! Let me out!

OLD MAN.   We'll send the baby after you in a ram's
skin.

PEER (*wipes the sweat from his brow*). I wish to God I
   could wake!

OLD MAN. Shall we send him to the palace?

PEER. Send him to the parish!

OLD MAN. Very well, Prince Peer. It's your affair.
   But one thing's certain. What's done is done.
   Your child will grow. And these mongrels shoot up
   Indecently fast—

PEER. Old man, now don't be a stubborn ox.
   Be reasonable, madam. Let's come to terms.
   [Whether you measure me or weigh me]
   You'll profit little by keeping me.
   The truth is I'm neither a prince nor rich.
   (*The* GREENCLAD ONE *collapses and is carried out by*
               TROLL MAIDENS.)

OLD MAN (*looks at him with deep disdain for a moment,
   then says*) Bash him to bits on the rocks, my
   children.

TROLL CHILDREN. Oh father, can't we play owl and
   eagle first?
   The wolf game? Grey mouse and fire-eyed cat?

OLD MAN. All right, but hurry. I'm out of temper
   And sleepy. Good night. (*Goes.*)

PEER (*as the* TROLL CHILDREN *chase him*). Let me go,
   you little beasts!
          (*Tries to climb up the chimney.*)

TROLL CHILDREN. Goblins! Elves! Bite him in the
   bottom!

PEER. Yow! (*Tries to get down through the cellar-
   flap.*)

TROLL CHILDREN. Close every crack!

OLDEST COURTIER. What fun they're having, the little
   dears!

PEER (*fighting with a* TROLL CHILD *which has fastened
   its teeth in his ear*). Get away, you little wretch!

OLDEST COURTIER (*strikes him across the fingers*). Brute!
   Learn to respect a royal child.

PEER. A rat-hole! (*Runs to it.*)

TROLL CHILDREN. Block it up, brother imp!

PEER. The old man was bad, but the young ones are worse!

TROLL CHILDREN. Tear him!

PEER. Oh, why aren't I the size of a mouse? (*Runs around.*)

TROLL CHILDREN (*milling around him*). Close the circle! Close the circle!

PEER (*weeps*). Why aren't I a louse? (*Falls.*)

TROLL CHILDREN. Now for his eyes!

PEER (*buried beneath the heap of* TROLL CHILDREN). Help! Mother! I'm dying!
    (*Church bells are heard tolling distantly.*)

TROLL CHILDREN. Bells on the mountain! The Black-Frock's cows!

(*The* TROLLS *flee in turmoil, yelling and screaming. The hall crashes in ruins. Everything disappears.*)

———————

Pitch darkness. PEER GYNT *is heard hewing and beating about with a great branch.*

PEER. Answer me! Who are you?

A VOICE IN THE DARK. Myself.

PEER. Get out of my way!

VOICE. Go round, Peer. The moor is big enough.

PEER (*tries to go through at another point, but is blocked by something*). Who are *you*?

VOICE. Myself. Can you say the same?

PEER. I can say what I like; my sword is sharp.
    Beware! Huh, hah, now it strikes and crushes!
    King Saul slew hundreds, Peer Gynt slays thousands!
                    (*Strikes and hews.*)
    Who *are* you?

VOICE. Myself.

PEER. You can keep that rubbish. It doesn't help.
  What are you?

VOICE. The Great Boyg.

PEER. Ah! Now I begin to understand.
  Out of my way, Boyg!

VOICE. Go round, Peer.

PEER. No, through! (*Hews and slashes.*)
  He's fallen! (*Tries to advance but comes up against
    something.*)
  Oh-ho! Are there more?

VOICE. The Boyg, Peer Gynt! One, only one.
  The Boyg that's unharmed, and the Boyg that you
    wounded.
  The Boyg that's dead, and the Boyg that is alive.

PEER (*throws down his branch*). My sword is troll-
    smeared; but I have my fists!
              (*Fights his way forward.*)

VOICE. Yes, trust to your fists. Trust to your strength.
  He-he, Peer Gynt. That's the way to the top.

PEER (*tries again*). Forward or back, it's equally far.
  Outside or in, I'm still confined.
  There he is! And *there!* And round that bend!
  As soon as I'm out I'm back in the middle,
  Encircled. Name yourself! Let me see you!
  What on earth are you?

VOICE. The Boyg.

PEER (*gropes around*). Not dead. Not alive. Slimy.
    Misty.
  And shapeless. [It's just like bumping around
  In a herd of growling, half-awake bears!]
              (*Shouts.*)
  Hit me back!

VOICE. The Boyg is no fool.

PEER. Strike!

VOICE. The Boyg does not strike.

PEER. Fight! You shall!

VOICE. The Great Boyg wins without fighting.

PEER. If only there were a goblin to prick me,
  Or even a baby troll!
  Something to fight! But there's nothing.
  Now he's snoring! Boyg!

VOICE. What do you want?

PEER. Use force!

VOICE. The Great Boyg wins by doing nothing.

PEER (*bites his own arms and hands*). Let me feel claws
    and teeth in my flesh!
  I must feel the drip of my own blood!
      (*The wing-beats of great birds are heard.*)

BIRD CRIES. Is he coming, Boyg?

VOICE IN THE DARK. Yes. Step by step.

BIRD CRIES. O Sisters, sisters far away!
  Fly hither! The time is come!

PEER. If you're going to save me, girl, do it quickly!
  Don't look at your lap, so humble and shy.
  Your prayer-book! Throw it in his eyes!

BIRD CRIES. He's swaying!

VOICE IN THE DARK. We have him.

BIRD CRIES. Sisters! Come quickly!

PEER. An hour of this consuming strife
  Is too dear a price to pay for life. (*Sinks to the ground.*)

BIRD CRIES. Boyg, he's fallen! Take him! Take him!
    (*The tolling of church bells and psalm song are heard
          in the distance.*)

THE BOYG (*shrinks to nothing, and gasps*). He was too
    strong. There were women behind him.

Sunrise. *On the mountain outside* AASE'S *saeter. The
door is shut. Everything is still and deserted.* PEER GYNT
is lying asleep outside the saeter wall.

PEER (*wakes and looks round dully and heavily. He spits*).
    Oh, for a salted herring![5]

(*Spits again. As he does so, he sees* HELGA *coming
with a hamper of food.*)

Hullo, child, are you here? What do you want?

HELGA. It's Solveig—

PEER (*jumps up*). Where is she?

HELGA. Behind the wall.

SOLVEIG (*hidden*). If you come near me, I'll run away!

PEER (*stops*). Are you afraid I'll kiss you?

SOLVEIG. For shame!

PEER. Do you know where I was last night?
  The Old Man of the Mountains' daughter
  Is after me everywhere like a gadfly.

SOLVEIG. Then it was lucky they rang the bells.

PEER. They can't fool Peer Gynt. Can they?

HELGA (*starts to cry*). Oh, she's running away!
              (*Runs after her.*)
  Wait!

PEER (*seizes her by the arm*). Look what I've got in my
      pocket!
  A silver button, child! You shall have it—
  Only say a good word for me.

HELGA. Let me go. Let me go!

PEER. Here it is.

HELGA. Let me go. There's the basket.

PEER. God have mercy on you if you don't—!

HELGA. Oh, you're frightening me!

PEER (*quietly, lets go of her*). No, I only meant—ask
      her not to forget me!

              (HELGA *runs away.*)

ACT THREE

Deep inside the pine forest. Grey autumn weather. Snow is falling. PEER GYNT *is standing in his shirtsleeves, felling timber.*

PEER *(hacks at a large fir-tree with twisted boughs).*
  Oh yes, you're tough, old friend. But it's no use.
  You're coming down.
                    (Hacks at it again.)
  You're wearing a chain shirt, are you?
  I'll cut through it. That's right,
  Yes, you can shake your twisted arm at me.
  I know you're angry.
  It can't be helped. I'll bring you to your knees—!
                    (Breaks off suddenly.)
  Lies! It's only an old tree!
  Bloody lies! It was never an armoured knight!
  [It's only a fir with crevices in its bark.
  It's heavy enough hewing timber,
  But hewing *and* dreaming—it's bloody murder!]
  I'm done with it, this living in mists and dreaming.
  You're an outlaw, my lad. They've hunted you into the
      woods.
                    (Hacks vigorously for a while.)
  Yes, an outlaw.
  You've no mother now to look after you.
  If you want to eat, you must help yourself,
  [Fetch it raw from the forest and river,
  Split your own wood and light your own fire.
  You'll have to start doing your own work now.]
  If you want a warm coat, you must shoot a deer.
  If you want a house you must break stones.

If you want walls, you must fell your own wood,
And carry it there upon your back.
(*His axe sinks to the ground. He stares unseeingly.*)
It'll be a grand sight! A tower with a weathercock
I'll have on the roof-beam! And I'll carve on the gable
A mermaid, shaped like a fish from her navel!
There'll be brass on the weathercock and all the locks.
And glass! I must try to have some of that!
Strangers will stare and wonder at it
Glittering there high on the hillside—
                         (*Laughs angrily.*)
Bloody lies! There they are again!
You're an outlaw, my lad.
                         (*Hacks fiercely.*)
                                      A bark-thatched hut
Will keep out the worst of the rain and frost.
[(*Looks up at the tree.*)
Now he's trembling. There! Just a kick
And he totters and measures his length on the ground,
The undergrowth milling and shuddering about him.
(*Begins to lop the branches.*)] (*Suddenly he listens
and stands still with his axe raised.*)
Someone's after me! [Is it Ingrid's father?
Old Heggstad gaffer! Ah, you'd cheat me, would you?]
      (*Ducks behind the tree and peeps round it.*)
[A boy. All alone. He seems to be frightened.
He glances around. What's he got hidden there
Under his jacket? A sickle. He stops and looks round.
Lays his hand flat on the rail of the fence.
What's this, now? Why is he suddenly swaying—?
Oh, my God! Why, he's chopped his finger off![6]
A whole finger! Right off! [He's bleeding like an ox!
Now he's running away with his hand in a clout!]
                         (*Gets up.*)
What a fool! An irreplaceable finger!
Right off! And of his own free will!
Ah! I see! That's the only way
To free oneself from serving the King.
That's it. They wanted to send him to the war

And the boy didn't want to go.
But to chop—? To lose for ever—?
Yes, to think—wish—to *will* it even;
But to *do* it! No, that I don't understand.
      (*Gives a little shake of his head,
        then returns to his work.*)

A room down at AASE'S *house. Everything is in disorder.
Boxes lie open, clothes are everywhere, a cat is on the
bed.* AASE *and* KARI, *a crofter's wife, are busy packing and
putting things in order.*

AASE (*runs over to one side of the room*).   Kari, come
    here!

KARI.   What is it?

AASE (*on the other side of the room*).   Come here—!
    Where is—? Where can I find—? Answer me! Where is
    the—?
    What am I looking for? I'm losing my wits.
    Where's the key to the chest?

KARI.   In the keyhole.

AASE.   What's that rumbling?

KARI.   The last waggon-load going off to Heggstad.

AASE (*weeps*).   I wish it was me they were taking away
    In a black box. Oh, the things a mortal
    Has to endure! God in His mercy help me!
    The whole house stripped!
    What the girl's father left, the bailiff's taken.
    They didn't spare the clothes on my back.
    Fie! The Devil rot them for being so hard!
          (*Sits on the edge of the bed.*)
    The land and the house are lost to our family.
    [The old man was harsh, but the law was harsher.]
    There was no help and no mercy.
    Peer was gone. I'd no-one to save me.

KARI.   At least you can stay in this room till you die.

AASE.   Yes; my cat and I will be fed by the parish.

KARI. God pity you, mother. Your Peer's cost you dear.

AASE. Peer? You're out of your mind!
Ingrid came safely home in the end.
It's the Devil they ought to blame. He's the villain
And no-one else. He led my boy astray.

KARI. Don't you think I'd better send for the priest?
[I'm fearing things may be worse than you know.]

AASE. The priest? Oh, yes, I almost think so.
                    (*Starts up.*)
But, oh God, no, I can't! I'm the lad's mother.
I must help him. It's my duty
To do what I can when the rest fail.
They've left him this coat. I must patch it up.
I wish I'd hidden the skin rug too.
Where are his stockings?

KARI. There, with the other rubbish.

AASE (*roots around*). What's this?
Oh, Kari, look! It's an old casting-ladle!
With this he played at being a button-moulder;
Melted and shaped and stamped.
One day at a feast, the little lad came
And asked his father for a lump of tin.
"Tin!", said John. "No! [Good King Christian's coin!]
Silver! Let people know you're John Gynt's son!"
God forgive the poor man, he was drunk,
And then he cared neither for tin nor gold.
Here are the stockings. Oh dear, they're all holes.
We must darn them, Kari.

KARI. I'm afraid so.

AASE. When it's done, I must get to bed.
I feel weak and wretched and frail.
(*Joyfully.*) Look, Kari! Two woollen shirts! They've
    missed them!

KARI. Yes, so they have.

AASE. What a piece of luck! You'd better hide one.
No, wait. I think we'll take both.
The one he's wearing is worn and thin.

KARI. God forgive you, Mother Aase! It's a sin!
AASE. And if it is? What's the priest for?
He'll pardon this sin, as he pardons others.

Outside a newly built cabin in the forest. A reindeer's antlers over the door. The snow is piled high around. It is twilight. PEER GYNT *is standing outside the door making fast a large wooden bolt.*

PEER (*laughing now and then*). I must have bolts!
Bolts against trolls, and against men and women.
[I must have bolts.]
Bolts to lock out all nagging hobgoblins.
They come with the darkness. They knock and they tap.
"Let us in, Peer Gynt! We're as swift as thoughts!
We scratch under the bed, we hiss in the ashes,
We breathe down the chimney like white-hot dragons!
He-he, Peer Gynt! Do you think nails and planks
Can shut out nagging hobgoblin thoughts?"

(SOLVEIG *comes over the heath on skis. She has a shawl over her head and a bundle in her hand.*)

SOLVEIG. God speed your work. Don't turn me away.
You sent for me, and so you must take me.
PEER. Solveig! It can't be—! Yes, but it is!
Aren't you afraid to come so near me?
SOLVEIG. You sent me a message by little Helga.
Others followed, in storm and in calm.
All that your mother said carried a message
That bred each morning as I awoke.
The lonely nights and the empty days
Bore me the message that now I must come.
It became as though life down there had been
    quenched.
I couldn't laugh or cry from my heart.
I didn't know how you felt about me.
I only knew what I had to do.
PEER. But your father?

SOLVEIG.   In all God's earth
  I have no-one to call father or mother.
  I have made myself free.

PEER.   Solveig, my fairest—to come to me?

SOLVEIG.   Yes, to you alone. You must be
  All to me. My friend and comforter.
                    [(*Weeps.*)
  The worst was to leave my little sister.
  But even worse to be parted from Father.
  But worst of all, to leave her who bore me at her breast.
  No, God forgive me, the worst was the grief
  At being parted from all of them—all of them.]

PEER.   You know the judgment read in the spring?
  I have lost my home and my inheritance.

SOLVEIG.   Do you think I left my dearest ones
  For the sake of an inheritance?

PEER.   —that anyone who meets me
  Outside the forest may freely seize me?

SOLVEIG.   I ran here on my skis. I asked my way.
  They said: "Where are you going?" I answered:
    "Home."

PEER.   Then to hell with nails and planks!
  Now I need no lock against hobgoblin thoughts!
  If you dare come in to live with the hunter
  I know that a blessing will fall on this house.
  Solveig! Let me look at you! Not too close!
  I just want to look at you. You're so bright and pure.
  Let me lift you. You're so delicate and light.
  Let me carry you, Solveig. I'll never get tired!
  I shall never soil you. I'll stretch out my arms
  And hold you from me, my fair, my warm one!
  Oh, who would have thought I could draw you to me?
  Oh, but I've longed for you night and day.
  Here you see I've been hewing and building.
  I must pull it down. It is mean and ugly—

SOLVEIG.   Mean or fine, it is what I want.
  Here one can breathe against the wind.
  Down there it was airless. I felt shut in.

[It was partly that that frightened me away.]
But here where I hear the fir tree whisper—
In stillness and song! Here I am at home!

PEER. Are you sure you want this? For the rest of your life?

SOLVEIG. I have chosen my path. I shall never turn back.

PEER. Then I have you! Go in! Let me see you inside!
I'll bring pine logs to make you a fire.
It will shine brightly and make you warm.
You shall sit softly and never be cold.

(*He opens the door.* SOLVEIG *goes in. He stands still for a moment, then laughs aloud with joy and jumps in the air.*)

PEER. My princess! Now at last I've found and won her!
Hey! Now I'll build my palace on firm, true ground!

(*He seizes the axe and walks away. As he does so, an* OLD-LOOKING WOMAN *dressed in green rags comes out of the trees. An* UGLY CHILD *with an ale-flagon in its hand limps after her, clutching her by the skirt.*)

WOMAN. Good evening, Peer Lightfoot!

PEER. What? Who are you?

WOMAN. Old friends, Peer Gynt.
My cottage lies nearby. We're neighbours.

PEER. Oh? That's news to me.

WOMAN. As you built your house, mine rose beside it.

PEER (*turns*). I'm in a hurry—

WOMAN. You always were, lad.
But I'll trudge behind, and one day I'll catch you.

PEER. You've made a mistake, grannie.

WOMAN. I did before.
I did when you made such promises to me.

PEER. I promised—? What damned nonsense is this?

WOMAN. Have you forgotten the night you drank
With my father? Have you forgotten—?

PEER. [I've only forgotten what I never knew.]
What are you talking about? When did we meet?

WOMAN. We last met when we first met.
> (*To the* CHILD.)
Give your father a drink. I dare say he's thirsty.

PEER. Father—? Are you drunk? Are you suggesting that
he—?

WOMAN. Can't you tell the pig by its skin?
Where are your eyes? Can't you see he's crippled
The way you're crippled, in your soul?

PEER. Are you trying to make me believe—?

WOMAN. Are you trying to deny it?

PEER. That long-legged brat—?

WOMAN. Yes, he's shot up quickly.

PEER. You damned troll-snout, do you dare to accuse
me—?

WOMAN. Wait a minute, Peer Gynt! I want none of your
insults.
> (*Weeps.*)
Can I help it if I'm not beautiful
As I was when you seduced me on the hillside?
Last fall, when I bore him, the Fiend gripped my back,
So it's not surprising I've become ugly.
But if you want to see me as fair as before
Just take that girl and show her the door.
Turn her out of your mind and out of your heart—
Do that, my dear, and I'll lose my snout.

PEER. Get away, you witch!

WOMAN. Yes, see if I do!

PEER. I'll split your skull—!

WOMAN. Try if you dare! Oh no, Peer Gynt.
I'm not frightened of blows. I'll come back every day.
I'll pull the door open and peer at you both.
When you're snuggling up to your girl on the hearth,
When you kiss her, Peer Gynt, when you'd pet her and
play with her,
I'll sit down beside you and demand my share.
She and I will take you by turns.
Goodbye, my love. You can marry tomorrow.

PEER. You hell-born nightmare—!

WOMAN. Oh, I nearly forgot.
You must raise the brat, you lecherous devil.
Come on, baby devil, go to your father.

CHILD (*spits at him*). [You keep away from me!]
I'll hit you with my axe! Just you wait! Just you wait!

WOMAN (*kisses the* CHILD). [You've a wise head on those
little shoulders.]
You'll be the spit of your father when you grow up.

PEER (*stamps his foot*). Would God you were as far—!

WOMAN. As we are near?

PEER (*clenches his fists*). And all this—!

WOMAN. For nothing but *thinking*?
It's bad luck on you, isn't it? Poor Peer!

PEER. It's worse for another.
O Solveig, my taintless, my purest gold!

WOMAN. Ah, well. It's the innocent who have to suffer;
As the Devil said when his mother hit him
Because his father was drunk.
(*She trudges off into the wood with the* CHILD, *who
throws the ale-flagon at* PEER.)

PEER (*after a long silence*). Go round, said the Boyg.
So I must here.
There falls my palace in ruins about me.
It's walled her round when I stood so near.
Everything here is suddenly ugly.
My joy has turned old. Go round, my lad.
There's no way straight through to her.
Straight? Hm, but there *should* be one.
[There's a text, if I remember aright—]
"If a man repent—". How does it go?
I've forgotten, and there's no-one here to guide me.
[Repent? It might take years to fight my way through.
That would be a poor life;
To smash what is pure, precious and beautiful,
And piece it together from broken fragments.
You can do that with a fiddle, but not with a bell.

Where the grass would grow green, one mustn't tread.
   But anyway, the witch was lying.]
They have gone. Gone, yes; but I can't forget them.
Tiptoeing thoughts will follow me in.
Ingrid! And those three that danced on the mountain!
Will they join me too? With cruel laughter
Demanding like her to be clasped in my arms?
To be gently lifted and lovingly laid
At arms' length? Go round, lad.
If my arm were as long as a pine tree's trunk
I fear even then I'd hold her too near
To set her down white and unstained as before.

   I must find some way round, so that if I gain nothing
At least I shan't lose. One must try to forget.
(*Goes a few steps towards the hut, but stops again.*)
To go in after this? So ugly and soiled?
To take in all those black trolls with me?
To speak, yet be silent? Confess, yet conceal—?
          (*Throws away his axe.*)
[It's a Sabbath evening.]
To keep tryst as I am would be sacrilege.

SOLVEIG (*in the doorway*). Are you coming?

PEER (*half to himself*). Round!

SOLVEIG. What did you say?

PEER. You must wait.
   It's dark, and I've something heavy to carry.

SOLVEIG. Wait. I'll help you. We'll share the burden.

PEER. No. Stay where you are. I must bear it alone.

SOLVEIG. Don't go too far, Peer.

PEER. Be patient.
   I may be long, but wait for me. Wait for me!

SOLVEIG (*nods after him*). Yes, I'll wait.

   (PEER *goes away down the forest path.* SOLVEIG *remains standing in the open half-door.*)

———

AASE'S *room. Evening. A log-fire is burning in the open hearth, and gives light to the room. The cat sits on a chair at the foot of the bed.* AASE *is lying in the bed, her hands moving restlessly on the coverlet.*

AASE. Oh, God! Won't he come? He's so long!
I've no-one to send and so much to say.
There's no time to lose. It's so quick!
Who'd have thought—? Oh, if only I knew
I'd not been too strict with the lad—!

PEER (*enters*). Hullo!

AASE. Oh, God bless you! You've come at last, my son.
But how dare you come down here?
Don't you know they're after your life?

PEER. My life can look after itself. I had to come to you.

AASE. Well, Kari was wrong. Now I can go in peace.

PEER. Go? Now what are you saying?
Where do you think you're going?

AASE. Oh, Peer, I'm near the end. I haven't much time left.

PEER (*squirms and walks up the room*). Oh, God! [I can't escape sorrow anywhere!]
I thought I'd be free from it here—! Are your feet and hands cold?

AASE. Yes, Peer. It'll soon be over. When you see
My eyes glaze, you must close them carefully.
And then you must see to the coffin. Now, my dear,
Be sure it's a fine one. Oh no, I'd forgotten—

PEER. Be quiet. There's time enough to think of that.

AASE. Yes, yes. (*Looks restlessly round the room.*)
This is all they left me. Just like them.

PEER (*writhes*). Again! (*In a hard voice.*)
I know it's my fault. Why remind me of that?

AASE. You? No, it's that damned liquor. [That's the cause
Of all the trouble.] My darling boy, you were drunk.
Then a man doesn't know what he's doing. Besides,

You'd been riding the stag. It's no wonder your head
    was turned.

PEER. [Yes, well, never mind that.]
Let's forget all that. Let's not be unhappy now.
        (*Sits on the edge of the bed.*)
Now, mother, let's chat together,
But only of little things.
Let's forget what's ugly and crooked,
And all that's painful and sore.
Look! The old cat! So he's still alive!

AASE. He howls so at night. You know what that means.

PEER (*changes the subject*). What's the news around
    here?

AASE (*smiles*). They say there's a girl who keeps her eyes
    Turned to the mountains—

PEER (*quickly*). Mads Moen, is he happy?

AASE. [They say she won't listen to her parents' tears.]
You ought to see them, Peer. [You might be able to
    help—]

PEER. Aslak the smith, what's happened to him?

AASE. Don't mention that rascal to me!
I'd rather tell you *her* name—

PEER. [No, mother, let's chat together,
But only of little things.
We'll forget what's ugly and crooked,
And all that's painful and sore.]
Are you thirsty? Can I fetch you a drink?
Can't you stretch your legs? This bed is short.
Let me see! Why, isn't this the bed
I slept in when I was a child?
Do you remember how often of an evening
You sat by my bedside and spread the fur rug over me
And sang me songs?

AASE. Yes, do you remember? When your father
Was away on a journey, we'd play sledges.
The rug was a sledge and the floor was an icebound
    fjord.

PEER. Yes, but the best of all—oh, mother,
Do you remember that too?—was the white horses!

AASE. [Of course I do!] Do you think I've forgotten that?
We'd borrow Kari's cat and sit it down on a chair—

PEER. To the castle west of the moon
And the castle east of the sun,
To Soria-Moria Castle
The road ran high and low!
We found a stick in a closet
And you used that as a whip—

AASE. I sat up here on the box-seat—

PEER. Yes, yes! You threw loose the reins
And kept turning round as we rode
To ask me if I was cold.
God bless you, ugly old mother!
You were always a loving soul!
Why are you crying?

AASE. It's my back. The hard board hurts it.

PEER. Stretch out, now. Let me settle you.
There, now you're lying softly.

AASE (*restlessly*). No, Peer. I want to go.

PEER. Go?

AASE. Yes, go. It's all I want.

PEER. What nonsense! Spread the rug over you.
Let me sit on the edge of the bed.
There! Now we'll shorten the evening with song.

AASE. No, get the prayer-book from the closet.
My soul's restless.

PEER. In Soria-Moria Castle[7]
The great King's giving a feast.
Rest there on the sledge-cushion, mother.
I'll drive you over the moor—

AASE. But Peer, have I been invited?

PEER. Yes, we both have been.

(*Throws a string round the chair on which the cat is sitting, takes a stick in his hand and sits on the foot of the bed.*)

Gee-up! Will you stir yourself, Grane![8]
Now, mother, you're sure you're not cold?
Oh, yes! You can feel you're speeding
Once Grane begins to go!

AASE. Peer dear, what's that ringing?

PEER. It's the silver sleigh-bells, mother!

AASE. Oh dear, what's that hollow rumbling?

PEER. We're driving over a fjord.

AASE. I'm frightened! What's that wild sighing?

PEER. It's the pine trees, mother, whispering on the moor.
Sit still, now—

AASE. There's something winking and sparkling in the distance.
Where's that light coming from?

PEER. From the windows and doors of the Castle.
Can you hear? They're dancing.

AASE. Yes.

PEER. St. Peter's standing outside. He's asking you to step in.

AASE. Is he speaking to us?

PEER. Yes, and he's taking his hat off. He's offering his sweetest wine.

AASE. Wine? Are there cakes too?

PEER. Oh, yes! A tasty plateful!
And the Bishop's wife is offering coffee and sweets.

AASE. Oh, Lord! Am I going to meet her?

PEER. As often as you wish, and as equals.

AASE. Oh Peer, what a spree you're taking my poor old bones on!

PEER (*cracks his whip*). Hey! Hup! Come on, rouse yourself, Grane!

AASE. Peer dear, are you driving carefully?

PEER (*cracks his whip again*). The road's broad here.

AASE. Don't drive so fast. I feel so old and tired.

PEER. I can see the Castle towering ahead of us.
  Our journey will soon be done.

AASE. I'll lie back and close my eyes,
  And trust in you, my son.

PEER. Gee-up now, Grane, my beauty!
  My word, the excitement is great!
  They've spotted Peer Gynt and his mother,
  And they're fighting to get to the gate!
  What's that you're saying, St. Peter?
  You won't let her in? My good sir,
  You can sit on your backside till Doomsday
  And you'll find no-one better than her.
  [I'm not going to boast of my virtues.
  I can turn and go back where I came.
  If you want me, I'll come in and thank you.
  If not, many thanks just the same.
  Sure, I've told as many lies as the Devil in any pulpit,
  And sworn at my mother and called her a bloody old
      hen
  Because she was always crowing and cackling at me.
  But] You see she's received with respect, mind.
  You make her feel really at home!
  She's the best soul you'll get from this parish.
  If you don't like her, go back to Rome!
  Ho-ho! Here comes God the Father!
  Now, St. Peter, we'll soon see who's who.
               (In a deep voice.)
  None of your bloody butler's airs, now.
  Just let Mother Aase come through.
         (Laughs aloud and turns to his mother.)
  There, isn't it just as I told you?
  That's made the old so-and-so run!
               (Frightened.)
  Why are you so silent, mother?
  Speak to me! It's Peer, your son!
               (Goes to the bed-head.)
  Don't lie there and stare at me, mother!
  Don't open your eyes so wide!

(*Feels her forehead and hands carefully. Then he throws the string on to the chair and says softly.*)

I see. You can rest now, Grane.

We've come to the end of our ride.

Thank you for all your days.

For your beatings and kisses, my dear.

But now you must thank me too.

      (*Presses his cheek against her mouth.*)

So; the driver has had his fare.

KARI (*enters*). Peer! Are you here? Then the worst of our troubles are over.

Dear God, how soundly she's sleeping! Or—is she—?

PEER. Hush. She is dead.

(KARI *weeps over the body.* PEER *walks round the room for a while. At length he stops by the bed.*)

PEER. See my mother is buried with honour.

I must get away from here.

KARI. Where are you going?

PEER. Seawards.

KARI. So far?

PEER. And far beyond.

           (*He goes.*)

ACT FOUR

On the southwest coast of Morocco. A palm grove. A table laid for dinner, with a sun awning and rush mats. Hammocks have been hung further back in the grove. Offshore lies a steam yacht flying the Norwegian and American flags. On the beach is a dinghy. It is towards sundown.

PEER GYNT, *a handsome middle-aged gentleman in elegant travelling clothes, with a gold lorgnette hanging from his waistcoat, is presiding as host at the dinner-table.* MR. COTTON, M. BALLON, HERR VON EBERKOPF *and* HERR TRUMPETERSTRAALE[9] *are finishing their meal.*

PEER. Drink, gentlemen! Man was made for pleasure.
  What's done is done; what's past is past concern.
  [What can I offer you?]

TRUMPETERSTRAALE. You're a superb host, Peer.

PEER. You must allow some credit to my wealth,
  My steward and my cook.

COTTON. Here's to the four of you!

BALLON. Monsieur, you have a *goût*, a *ton*,
  Such as one seldom finds today
  Among men living *en garçon*.
  A certain—*qu'est-ce qu'on dit—?*

VON EBERKOPF.[10]   A measure
  Of spiritual contemplation,
  [A marvellous lack of chauvinism,
  A vision that can pierce the fog
  Of prejudice,] the ability
  To grasp Truth in its higher aspects—
  [Added to which] an *Ur-Natur*,
  [An unspoilt nature, all this crowned]

With a fine wealth of worldly knowledge—
Mein herr, was that not what you meant?

BALLON. *C'est bien possible.* [It doesn't sound
Quite so *magnifique* in French.]

VON EBERKOPF. [*Ei was!* Your language is so stiff.] But if
We wish to find the cause of the phenomenon—

PEER. It's easy. I've never married.
[Why, gentlemen, it is as clear as daylight.]
What should a man be? Himself. [That's all.]
He must live for himself and himself alone.
How can he if he spends his life
[Playing the pack-camel to a wife and children,]
Carrying the woes of others?

VON EBERKOPF. But to achieve this independence
You must have had to pay a price—

PEER. Oh, yes. Indeed—when I was young.
[But I always emerged an honourable victor.]
Once I was very nearly trapped.
I was a gay and good-looking boy
And the lady to whom I lost my heart
Was of royal birth—

BALLON. Royal?

PEER (*nonchalantly*). One of those ancient mountain
     families—
You know—

TRUMPETERSTRAALE (*thumps the table*). Aristocrats!

PEER (*shrugs his shoulders*). Degenerate idiots, who
     count it their chief pride
To keep plebeian stains from the family escutcheon.

COTTON. The romance fell through?

BALLON. Her family opposed the match?

PEER. On the contrary.

BALLON. Ah!

PEER (*forbearingly*). Well, there were circumstances,
You understand, that made it desirable
That we should marry with all decent speed.
But frankly, I found the whole business

From first to last somewhat unappetising.
In certain respects I'm a fastidious man.
[And I always like to stand on my own feet.]
So when her father started dropping hints
That I should change my name and my profession
And take out a licence of nobility,
With other suggestions that were equally
Distasteful, not to say unacceptable,
[I bowed my thanks, rejected his ultimatum
And renounced my youthful bride.]
(*Drums with his fingers on the table and looks pious.*)
Yes, yes; there's a destiny that shapes our ends.
[We mortals can safely put our trust in it.]
It's a great comfort to know it.

BALLON. That was the end of the affair?

PEER. Oh, no. Far from it. [Various outsiders
Poked in their noses and created mischief.
Her brothers and cousins were the worst.]
I had to fight duels with seven of them.
[It was a time I shall never forget.]
But I survived with honour. [It cost me blood.
However, that same blood attests my worth.
And is a further proof that our lives are ruled
By that wise fate of which I spoke just now.]

VON EBERKOPF. You have an outlook upon life
Which entitles you to be called a Philosopher.
[Where ordinary mortals guess,
Seeing each detail separately,
For ever groping, you are able
Fully to integrate your vision.
Measuring life by an unchanging norm
You gather scattered inspirations
So that they radiate like beams
Of one supreme philosophy.]
And you've never been to University?

PEER. [As I've told you before,] I am a self-taught man.
[I've studied nothing methodically.]
But I've thought and [speculated and] read a little

About most things. I started late in life.
[And, you know, it becomes a trifle wearisome
To plough through page after page, trying to absorb
What's dull with what is lively.]
I've learned my history by fits and starts.
It was all I had time for.
And since one must have some spiritual security
[To put one's trust in when times are hard]
I read religion—intermittently.
[That way it's easier to digest.
One shouldn't read to gulp down everything.]
One must select [what one will be able to use.]

COTTON.   Very practical.

PEER *(lights a cigar)*.   My dear friends,
Consider my own career. What was I
When I came to the West? A penniless lad.
I had to sweat to earn my bread.
Believe me, things were very hard.
But life, my friends, is sweet; and death is bitter.
Fortune smiled upon me, as you see.
[And old man Fate was tolerant.] I prospered.
[And, since my own philosophy was elastic,
Things went from good to better.] Within ten years
The Charleston ship-owners were calling me Croesus.
My fame spread from port to port. Luck sat in my
    sails—

COTTON.   What did you carry?

PEER.   Mostly negro slaves to Carolina,
And heathen images to China.

BALLON.   *Fi donc!*

TRUMPETERSTRAALE.   My dear sir—!

PEER.   You think it was a trifle unethical?
I felt the same myself—oh, very keenly.
I may even say I hated it.
But believe me, once you've begun, it's hard to stop.
And I didn't want to create unemployment.
[In so gigantic an enterprise as this

Which keeps whole thousands in employment,
It's very hard to call things to a halt
For good. "For good." I can't abide those words.
On the other hand, I must confess
I've always had the healthiest respect
For what men call the consequences.
And the prospect of overstepping the mark
Has always induced a certain timidity in me.]
Well, I was beginning to grow old;
[Approaching fifty. My hair was turning grey.]
And though my health was excellent, one thought
     haunted me:
"Who knows how soon the hour of judgment will strike?
[And the great judgment separate sheep from goats.]"
What could I do?
To stop the China trade was impossible.
But I found a solution. [I quickly opened
Another trade with the same country.]
Each spring I sent them idols, and each autumn
Exported missionaries, generously equipped
With woollen stockings, Bibles, rice and rum—

COTTON. At a profit, I presume?

PEER. Of course. [This enterprise
Also prospered. They worked indefatigably.]
For every idol that I sold
They got a coolie honestly baptised.
Thus the effect was neutralised.
[The field of holy work never lay fallow,
The idols being countered by the missionaries.]

COTTON. But what about your African cargoes?

PEER. There too my sense of morality triumphed.
[I realised it was a foolish traffic
For one advanced in years. One never knows
When the summons to judgment may come.
Besides, there were the patrol boats
Not to mention the philanthropists
And the risks of wind and weather.
All these considerations won the day.]

"Peter," I said, "it's time to reef your sails.
You must right your wrongs."
I purchased a plot of land in the South,
And kept the last cargo [which happened
To be of the primest quality,] for myself.
They flourished, and grew [sleek and] fat,
Giving the highest satisfaction
Both to themselves and me. Indeed,
I think I can say without boasting, I was
A father to them. And reaped my just reward.
[I built schools, and kept the strictest watch
To ensure the maintenance of morality.]
And now I have withdrawn from the whole concern.
I've sold the plantation, with all its stock
Of hide and hair. [The day I left
I gave to every man, woman and child
Grog, *ad lib* and *gratis;* so that they all got drunk,
And every widow had an ounce of snuff.]
So surely, [if] the old saying holds true:
"Who doeth not evil worketh good"
[The follies of my past are now forgotten,
And, more than most men, I can safely claim
That my good deeds are weightier than my sins].

VON EBERKOPF (*clinks glasses with him*). It is wonderful
        to meet a man
Who lives according to his principles.
[Uninhibited by foggy theories,
Immutable in the face of outward chaos.]

PEER (*who during the preceding dialogue has been help-
        ing himself steadily from the various bottles*).
[We Northern warriors know how to carry a battle
Through to its harsh conclusion.] The key to life
Is simply this. Close your ear against
The infiltration of a dangerous serpent.

COTTON.   What serpent, my good friend?

PEER.   A little one that is most seductive.
The one that tempts you to commit yourself.
                    (*Drinks again.*)

The art of success is to stand free
And uncommitted amid the snares of life.
To know that the day of battle is not the day
Of judgment. There are other days to come.
To know that a bridge always remains open
Behind you. That theory has shaped my whole career.
[This theory is a national inheritance.
I entered into it in my parents' home.

BALLON. You're Norwegian, aren't you?

PEER. By birth. But cosmopolitan by temperament.
For my success I'm indebted to America.
For my book-learning to the new German schools.
From France I have acquired my waistcoat here,
My manners, and the little wit I own.
From England I have learned industriousness
And a quick eye for opportunity.
The Jew has taught me patience, and Italy
Gave me a taste for *dolce far niente*.
And once, in an awkward situation,
I lengthened the measure of my days
With the help of Swedish steel.

TRUMPETERSTRAALE (*raises his glass*). Ah! Swedish
steel!]

VON EBERKOPF. Let us raise our glasses to the free
man!
(*They clink glasses with him and drink. He begins
to grow a little tipsy.*)

COTTON. All this is fine. Fine.
But tell me, sir, I'm curious to know
What you propose to do with all your money.

PEER. Hm! Do with it? Eh?

ALL FOUR (*edge closer*). Yes! Tell us!

PEER. Well, first of all
I want to travel. That's why I took you aboard
As travelling companions in Gibraltar.
I needed a chorus of friends to dance
Around the altar of my golden calf.

[VON EBERKOPF. Very witty.]

COTTON.　But no one sails merely for pleasure.
　You must have a goal. What is it?

PEER.　To become Emperor.

ALL FOUR.　What?

PEER (*nods*).　Emperor.

ALL FOUR.　Of what? Where?

PEER.　Of the whole world.

BALLON.　But how, my friend—?

PEER.　By the power of gold. It's not a new idea.
　The thought of it has been with me all my journey.
　When I was a child, I rode in my dreams
　Far over the ocean on a cloud.
　I soared with a host of men behind me,
　[And a golden scabbard]. But I fell
　Flat on my face. But that remained my goal.
　Someone—I forget who it was—once said
　That if you gain the whole wide world
　But lose yourself, your victory
　Is but a wreath about a cloven brow.
　[Those were the words, or something similar.]
　It's the truth.

VON EBERKOPF.　But who *is* your self?

PEER.　The world behind my forehead's vaulted arch,
　By cause of which I am myself alone,
　[And no one else, any more than God is Satan].

TRUMPETERSTRAALE.　Now I get it!

BALLON.　Sublime *penseur!*

VON EBERKOPF.　Most mighty poet!

PEER (*with increasing passion*).　My self—it is the army
　Of wishes, appetites, desires,
　[The sea of whims, pretensions and demands,]
　All that swells here within my breast
　And by which I, myself, exist.
　But, as Our Lord has need of common clay
　To make Him omnipotent, so I need gold
　To make me Emperor.

BALLON.　But you have gold.

PEER. Not enough. [Yes, perhaps for a nine days' wonder;
As Emperor *à la* Lippe-Detmold[11].
But I must be myself entirely;
Every inch a Gyntish inch,
From top to toe, Sir Peter Gynt.

BALLON (*carried away*). Possess the loveliest woman on
earth!

VON EBERKOPF. Your *Reich* last for a thousand years![12]

TRUMPETERSTRAALE. Stand in history with Charlemagne![13]

COTTON. Aye. But first may you find a profitable opening—

PEER. I have found it. Thanks to our anchoring here!]
This evening we sail northward. [The newspapers
I received on board brought tidings of importance;]
(*Gets up and raises his glass.*)

Dame Fortune ceaselessly assists the brave.

ALL FOUR. What? Tell us!

PEER. Greece is in revolt!

ALL FOUR (*jump up*). What? The Greeks!

PEER. They have risen against their masters.

ALL FOUR. Hurrah!

PEER. And the Turkish army is in confusion.
(*Empties his glass.*)

BALLON. To Hellas! The gate of glory is thrown wide!
[I'll help them with my Gallic rapier!

VON EBERKOPF. And I with fearful war-cries—from a distance.

COTTON. I, too, with arms. On pre-payment, of course.

TRUMPETERSTRAALE. Lead on! I'll find in Bender to as-
sist them
The famous buckles of King Charles's spurs!][14]

BALLON (*falls on* PEER GYNT'S *neck*). Forgive me, *mon
ami*, that I misjudged you!

VON EBERKOPF (*presses his hand*). Stupid dog that I am,
I took you for a scoundrel.

COTTON. Not as bad as that. A fool, perhaps—

TRUMPETERSTRAALE (*tries to kiss him*). [I took you,
Uncle, for an example
Of the worst kind of rotten Yankee brood.]
Forgive me—

VON EBERKOPF. [We have all been groping in the dark.]

PEER. What's all this?

VON EBERKOPF. [Now we see the whole Gyntish host
Of wishes, passions and desires
Most gloriously assembled—]

BALLON (*admiringly*). So *this* is being Monsieur Gynt!

VON EBERKOPF (*similarly*). This is to be Peer Gynt with
honour!

PEER. But please tell me—?

BALLON. You don't understand?

PEER. No, I'll be hanged if I do.

BALLON. What! But surely you are on your way
To help the Greeks with ships and money?

PEER (*snorts*). No, thank you! I side with strength.
I am lending money to the Turk.

BALLON. Impossible!

VON EBERKOPF. Very witty. You're joking.

PEER (*is silent for a moment, then leans against a chair
and assumes a lofty mien*). Gentlemen, it is best
we part [before
The last shreds of friendship flicker away like smoke.]
The empty-fisted are always rash to gamble.
[The man who scarcely owns the strip of earth
His shadow covers, is natural cannon fodder.]
But when a man is as rich as I am,
He has much to lose.
Go to Hellas. I will arm you *gratis*,
And set you safe ashore. The more you fan
The flames of patriotism, the more I have
To gain. Stand up for freedom! Fight for justice!
[Charge! Storm onwards! Stoke up hell for the Turk!]
And gloriously end your days

Upon the lances of the Janissaries!
But please excuse me. (*Slaps his pocket.*) I have gold,
And am myself, Sir Peter Gynt.
(*Opens his sunshade and goes into the grove, where
the hammocks can be glimpsed.*)

TRUMPETERSTRAALE. The darned swine!

BALLON. No sense of honour!

COTTON. To hell with honour!
Think of the profit if the Greeks should win!

BALLON. [I saw myself wreathed with the victor's gar-
land,
Surrounded by beautiful Grecian maidens.

TRUMPETERSTRAALE. I saw the spurs of Charles the
Twelfth
Resting where they belong, in Swedish hands.

VON EBERKOPF. I saw my fatherland's prodigious Kultur
Spreading itself over land and sea.

COTTON. It's the material loss that bothers me.
Goddamit! I could weep real tears.
I saw myself as the master of Olympus,
And if that mountain's reputation is correct
There are copper mines to be found there
Which I could open up and work afresh.
And that river Kastale they talk so much about—
All those waterfalls must at the lowest calculation
Be worth over a thousand horse-power—]

TRUMPETERSTRAALE. I shall go, nevertheless. [My Swedish sword
Is worth twice as much as Yankee gold.

COTTON. Possibly. But if we merely join the ranks
We'll be swallowed up with the rest. And where will
our profit be then?

BALLON. *Mon Dieu!* To climb so near success—!
And then to find oneself standing by its grave!]

COTTON (*shakes his fist towards the yacht*). And that
black coffin holds all the gold
That blasted Nabob sweated from his niggers.

VON EBERKOPF. An inspiration! What are we waiting for?
His empire lies within our grasp. Hurrah!

BALLON. What are you going to do?

VON EBERKOPF. Perform a *coup!* We have only to
bribe the crew,
[Which won't be difficult] and the yacht is ours.
Aboard!

COTTON. You mean *you—?*

VON EBERKOPF. I bag the whole caboodle. (*Goes down
to the dinghy.*)

COTTON. I can't neglect my own interests.
I'd better do the same.

TRUMPETERSTRAALE. The scoundrels!

BALLON. A bad business. *Mais enfin—* (*Follows the
others.*)

TRUMPETERSTRAALE. I suppose I shall have to join them.
But under protest![15] (*Follows.*)

---

*Another part of the coast. Moonlight and drifting
clouds. The yacht, a long way offshore, is under full steam.*
PEER GYNT *is running along the shore, now pinching his
arm, now staring out to sea.*

PEER. I'm dreaming! It's a nightmare! I'll wake up
soon.
She's sailing away! And at full steam!
It's a hallucination! I'm asleep! I'm drunk! I'm mad!
(*Clenches his fists.*)
I can't be going to die!
(*Tears his hair.*)
It's a dream. I insist it's a dream.
Oh, this is dreadful! It's only too real! What monsters!
Hear me, O Lord! You're so wise and so just! Judge!
(*Stretches up his arms.*)
It's me, Peter Gynt! Oh God, do pay attention!

Protect me, Father, or I must perish!
Make them turn the ship! Make them lower the sails!
Stop the thieves! Make something go wrong!
Oh, listen to me! Never mind other people.
The world can take care of itself for a while.
No, he's not listening. He's deaf as usual.
That's charming! A God who won't help when you need
    him.
             (*Waves upwards.*)
Psst! I've given up that nigger plantation!
I've sent missionaries all the way to China.
Surely one good turn is worth another!
Oh, please help me to get on board—!

(*A jet of flame shoots into the air from the yacht, and
thick smoke belches forth. A hollow explosion is heard.
PEER GYNT utters a shriek and sinks down on to the sand.
Gradually the smoke dissipates. The ship has vanished.*)

PEER (*pale and quiet*). The sword of vengeance!
Gone to the bottom with every soul on board!
Oh, what luck, what—!
             (*Moved.*)
Luck? No, it was more than that.
I was fated to be saved, and they to die.
O all thanks and praise to Thee for preserving me
In spite of all my sins!
            (*Emits a deep breath.*)
What a wonderful feeling of peace and safety it gives
To know that one is under special protection!
But the desert! What about food and drink?
Oh, I'll find something. He'll see to that.
There's no need to be afraid.
            (*Loudly and ingratiatingly.*)
He won't want a poor little sparrow like me
To perish. Just be humble. And give Him time.
Trust in the Lord and keep your courage up.
            (*Gives a frightened jump.*)
Was that a lion growling in the reeds?
            (*His teeth chatter.*)

No, it wasn't a lion.
> (*Plucks up his courage.*)

[Well, what's a lion?
Those beasts know it's best to keep out of the way
And not try to mix things with their betters.
Their instinct tells them not to play with elephants.]
Still, I'd better find a tree. There's a grove
Of palms and acacias over there.
If I get up in them I'll be safe and cool.
If only I knew a psalm or two!
> (*Climbs up into a tree.*)

["Morning is morning and night is night."
That's a text that has often been weighed and sifted.
> (*Seats himself more comfortably.*)

How splendid to feel so spiritually uplifted.
Noble thoughts are more than silk and pearls.]
Just trust in him. [He knows how much
Of the chalice of suffering I have strength to drink.]
He keeps a fatherly eye on me.
> (*Throws a glance out to sea and
> whispers with a sigh.*)

But he certainly isn't economical!

---

*Night. A Moroccan encampment on the edge of the
desert. Watch fires.* WARRIORS *resting.*

A SLAVE (*enters, tearing his hair*).   The Emperor's white
   charger is missing!

A SECOND SLAVE (*enters rending his clothes*).   The Emperor's sacred robes have been stolen!

AN OVERSEER (*enters*).   A hundred lashes of the bastinado
   For every man who fails to catch the thief!
> (THE WARRIORS *mount their horses and
> gallop off in all directions.*)

Dawn. The grove of palms and acacias. PEER GYNT, *up in his tree with a broken branch in his hand, is trying to ward off a swarm of monkeys.*

PEER.   Damnation! A most unpleasant night!
                    (*Beats around.*)
Monkeys!
You again! This is the bloody limit.
Now they're throwing fruit. No, it isn't fruit.
Filthy beasts! [How does the saying go?
"Thou shalt keep watch and fight." Well, I'm damned
     if I can.
My eyes feel like lead.]
     (*They disturb him again. He says impatiently.*)
I must put a stop to this. I must try to catch
One of the brats and [hang him and] skin him
And dress myself up in his hairy coat,
So the others will think I'm one of them.
What are we mortals? Just motes of dust.
We've got to adapt ourselves a little.
Another crowd of them. Milling and swarming!
Be off with you! Shoo! They're acting like lunatics.
If only I had a false tail now,
Or something that made me a bit like an animal.
What now? Something's rustling over my head—
                    (*Glances up.*)
It's the grandfather, with his fists full of filth—
(*Huddles nervously and keeps still for a moment. The monkey makes a movement.* PEER *begins coaxing him and talking to him gently as though to a dog.*)
Hullo, old boy, is that you up there?
You're clever, aren't you? [You know what's what.]
You're not going to throw—no, of course you're not.
It's me. Pip-pip! We're good friends, aren't we?
                    (*Gives a couple of squeaks.*)
Do you hear, I can talk your language!
We're relatives. Tomorrow morning
I'll give you some sugar—! You filthy brute!
The whole lot down on my head! Ugh! Disgusting!

Or perhaps it was food. (*Tastes.*) I'm not sure.
But taste is a question of what you are used to.
[Who was it that said: "One must spit and trust
In the power of habit"?] Oh, here come the young ones!
                    (*Beats around.*)
This is really too much, that Man, Lord of Creation,
Should be compelled to—! No, stop it! Curse!
The old one was bad, but the young ones are worse!

---

*Early morning. A stony landscape, with a view over
the desert. On one side a cleft in the mountain and a
cave. A* THIEF *and a* RECEIVER *are in the cleft with the
Emperor's horse and cloak. The horse, richly caparisoned,
is tied to a stone. Horsemen can be heard in the distance.*

THIEF.   The tongues of the lances
Are licking and playing.
See! See!

RECEIVER.   I can see my head
Roll in the sand!
Woe! Woe!

THIEF (*crosses his arms over his breast*).   My father was
      a thief
So his son must steal.

RECEIVER.   My father was a receiver,
So I must receive.

THIEF.   Thou must bear thy lot.
Thou must be thyself.

RECEIVER (*listens*).   Footsteps [among the stones]!
We must fly. But whither?

THIEF.   The cave is deep
And the Prophet is great.
(*They flee, leaving their loot behind them. The
sound of horsemen dies away in the distance.*)

PEER (*enters, cutting a reed pipe*).   What a beautiful
morning!

The dung-beetle's rolling his ball in the sand.
The snail is creeping out of his house.
Morning! Oh yes, it has gold in its mouth.
Daylight has a wonderful power.
One feels so safe, one's courage rises.
I could fight a bull!
Such silence everywhere! [Yes, these rustic pleasures!
How extraordinary that I ever came to reject them.
That man should choose to shut himself up in a city
And be pestered by crowds on his doorstep.]
The lizard darts around, snapping and thinking of
    nothing.
What innocence in the life of beasts!
Each is himself, obeying his Maker's purpose;
[Preserving unspoiled his characteristic essence,
And being himself, whether playing or fighting,
As on the day when God first commanded: "Be!"]
        (*Fixes his lorgnette on his nose.*)
A toad. In the middle of a [sandstone] rock.
[Stone all around him. Only his head is visible.]
There he sits, staring at life as through a window;
Being himself, and himself alone—!
Himself and himself alone! Who said that?
[I expect I read it when I was a boy,
In some so-called great book.] Was it the Prayer Book?
[Or Solomon? Bad.] Every year my memory gets worse.
        (*Sits down in the shade.*)
[Here's a cool place to rest and stretch my feet.
What's this? Ferns? Hm. Edible roots.
        (*Tastes them.*)
They're probably all right for animals.
But it is written: "Subdue thy nature,"
And also: "He that is proud shall be brought low,
And he that abaseth himself shall be exalted."
        (*Uneasily.*)
Exalted? Yes, that'll happen to me.
I can't see any other solution.
Providence will help me to escape from this country
And arrange for me to continue on my way.

This is merely a trial. Salvation will follow,
Provided only the good Lord grants me strength.
    (*Puts these thoughts aside.*] *Lights a cigar,
    stretches himself and gazes out over the desert.*)
What a vast and limitless waste!
Far away over there an ostrich is strutting.
What is one to believe was God's intention
In creating all this emptiness and death?
[This desert, devoid of all sources of life,
Burnt and yielding profit to no man.
This fragment of the world, for ever fallow.
This corpse that, never since the earth was born,
Has given its Creator as much as thanks.
Why was it made?] Nature is unpractical.
Is that the sea shining over there in the east?
Glittering—? No, it can't be. It's a mirage.
The sea's in the west behind me,
Dammed from the desert by a range of hills.
                (*A thought strikes him.*)
Dammed? I wonder—? Those hills are narrow.
Dammed? A little dynamite, a canal,
And the waters would rush like a life-giving river
In through the gap and fill the desert.
Soon this whole white-hot grave would lie
Fresh as a dimpled sea.
The oases would rise out of it like islands.
[Atlas grow green like our mountains in the north.]
The schooners, like migrating birds,
Would cut their way southwards on the caravan routes.
[The air of life will scatter these stuffy vapours,
And dew drop from the clouds.] Towns will arise,
And grass will grow around the swaying palms.
[The land to the south behind the Sahara's wall
Will become the coastland of a vital culture.
Steam will drive factories in Timbuctoo,
Bornu will speedily be colonised,
And scientists ride in their *wagons-lit*
Through Abyssinia to the Upper Nile.]

And in the midst of my sea, on a rich oasis,
I shall personally propagate the Norwegian race.
[The blood of our Northern valleys is—well, nearly
     royal,
And a little Arab mixture will do the rest.
Around a bay on rising sand
I'll found my capital, Peeropolis.]
The world's degenerate. Now comes the turn
Of Gyntiana,[10] my new land!
                    (*Jumps to his feet.*)
A little money and I could do it!
A golden key to the gate of the sea!
A crusade against Death! That mean old skinflint
Shall open the sack he lies brooding on!
[In every land the cry goes up for freedom.
Like the ass in the Ark I'll send my clarion call
Across the world, and bring the baptism of liberty
To the beautiful prisoned coasts that shall be born!]
I must do it! I must find capital!
My kingdom—well, half my kingdom for a horse!
                    (*The horse neighs in the cave.*)
A horse! And robes! And jewels! And a sword!
                    (*Goes closer.*)
It can't be. [Yes, it is. But—? I have read
Somewhere, that human will can move mountains.
But a horse too—!] Well, it's a fact, here stands the
     horse.
[*Ab esse ad posse, etcetera, etcetera*]
     (*Puts on the cloak and looks himself up and down.*)
Sir Peter. A Turk from top to toe!
No, one never knows what fate will bring?
Gee-up now, Crane, my trusty steed!
                    (*Mounts into the saddle.*)
Golden stirrups! But of course
You can tell a great man by the cut of his horse!
                    (*Gallops away into the desert.*)

———————

The tent of an Arab chieftain, alone in an oasis. PEER
GYNT, *in Oriental costume, is reclining on cushions, drinking coffee and smoking a long pipe.* ANITRA *and a group of
girls are dancing and singing for him.*

CHORUS OF GIRLS.   The Prophet is come!
The Prophet, the Master, [the Omniscient].
To us is he come,
[Riding across the ocean of the sand.
The Prophet, the Master, the Infallible,
To us, to us is he come,]
Through the sand-ocean sailing.
[Let flute and drum hail him;]
The Prophet, the Prophet is come.

ANITRA.   [His charger is white as the milk
That flows in the river of Paradise.]
Bend the knee! Bow the head!
His eyes are stars, shining and mild.
[But no earthborn child can endure
The brilliance of their light.]
Through the desert he came.
[Gold and pearls sprang forth on his breast.]
Where he rode, there was light.
Behind him all grew dark.
[Behind him drought and sandstorm reigned.]
He came, the Glorious One,
[Through the desert he came]
Dressed like a mortal.
[Kaba,17] Kaba stands empty.
He himself hath proclaimed it.

CHORUS OF GIRLS.   [Let flute and drum hail him.]
The Prophet, the Prophet is come.
                    (*The* GIRLS *dance to soft music.*)
PEER.   [I have read in print, and it's perfectly true:
"No man is a prophet in his own country."]
This is the life for me! [It's much better
Than the one over there among the Charleston ship-
    pers.
There was something hollow about all that,

Something foreign to me, something fishy behind it.]
I never felt at home among those shippers.
I never felt I was one of them.
Why did I ever get on to that waggon
To root around in the garbage cans of commerce?
[Now I think about it, I can't imagine why.
It just happened that way. That's the only answer.
    To be oneself by the power of gold
Is simply to build one's house upon sand.
If you've a gold watch and a diamond ring
People will fawn and grovel before you.
They'll raise their hats to your glittering tiepin
But the ring and the pin are not the man.]
A prophet's position is much clearer.
[You know where you are. If you're a success]
It's you that they worship and not your money.
[One is what one is, and no nonsense about it.
One isn't a debtor to Chance or Fate,
And one has no need of licence or patent.
To be a prophet. That's something for me.]
And I tumbled into it quite by chance.
Simply galloping through the desert
I stumbled upon these children of nature.
    Their Messiah had come; it was clear; [there was no
        doubt about it.]
I had no intention of deceiving them.
Prophetic utterances are not lies.
Besides, I can always revise my interpretations.
[I'm not bound at all. Things aren't too bad.
It's all a perfectly private matter.]
If it comes to the worst, I can leave as I came.
My horse stands ready.
In short, I am master of the situation.

ANITRA (*approaches*). Prophet and Master!

PEER. What would my slave?

ANITRA. The sons of the desert wait outside.
They beg to be allowed to see thy face.

PEER. Stop! Tell them to keep their distance.

Tell them I shall hear their prayers from there.
No men are allowed in here.
Men, my child, are a most untrustworthy race.
Miserable bastards! You can't imagine, [Anitra,]
How they have cheated—hm—sinned, my child.
Well, that's all over. You may dance for me, maidens.
The Prophet would forget such painful memories.

CHORUS (*dancing*).   The Prophet is good. The Prophet is
      grieved
At the evil the sons of the dust have committed.
The Prophet is merciful. Praised be his mercy!
He opens to sinners the portals of Paradise.

PEER (*his eyes follow* ANITRA *as she dances*).   [Her legs
      are as neat and nimble as drumsticks.]
Mm. She's a nice piece of delicatessen, that girl.
[A trifle extravagantly moulded. Not quite
The classical formula. But what is Beauty?
A mere convention. It changes like coin
From country to country and age to age.
But a little excess is a pleasant change
When one's drunk normality to the dregs.
You can't get intoxicated by what's average.
They're either too fat or too thin, or else
Disturbingly young or disgustingly old.
And what lies between seems insipid.]
Her feet aren't quite clean; nor are her arms.
Especially one. Still, that's no great defect.
It's almost an extra qualification.
Anitra, my child! Listen to me.

ANITRA (*approaches*).   Thy handmaiden listens.

PEER.   My child, you attract me. The Prophet is stirred.
If you don't believe me, I shall give you proof.
I'll make you a Houri in Paradise.

ANITRA.   Impossible, Lord.

PEER.   What? You think I'm joking?
I mean it, as truly as I am alive.

ANITRA.   But I have no soul.

PEER. That can be arranged.

ANITRA. How, Lord?

PEER. You leave that to me.
[I shall make it my personal task to educate you.
No soul! Yes, indeed, you are, as the saying goes,
Somewhat stupid. I've noticed it with distress.
But] the meanest creature has room for a soul.
Come here. Let me measure the size of your brain.
There's room, there's room. I knew I was right.
[You'll never become a profound thinker.]
Not very much room. Your soul will be small.
But what of that? You'll have enough.

ANITRA. The Prophet is good—

PEER. You hesitate? Answer!

ANITRA. I'd rather—

PEER. Speak out. Don't be afraid.

ANITRA. I don't mind so much about a soul.
I'd rather have—

PEER. What?

ANITRA (*points at his turban*). That beautiful opal.

PEER (*enraptured, hands her the jewel*). Anitra! O thou
    true daughter of Eve!
How can I refuse you? I am but a man.
[And, as a distinguished author has written:
"*Das ewig weibliche ziehet uns an!*"[18]]

———

A *moonlit night. A palm grove outside* ANITRA's *tent.*
PEER GYNT *is seated beneath a tree with an Arabian lute
in his hand. His hair and beard are clipped, and he looks
noticeably younger.*

PEER (*plays and sings*). I locked the gate of Paradise
    And took away its key.
I sailed towards the Southern Cross
While lovely women mourned their loss
On the salt shore of the sea.

South like a bird I sped my way
On wings of swift desire.
At last, where palm trees proudly sway
In a green wreath around the bay,
I set my ship on fire.

[I stepped aboard the desert ship,
A four-legged bold corsair.
Beneath my whip it skimmed along.
O, catch me! I'm a bird in song,
A-twittering in the air.]

Anitra, thou art the palm-tree's sap,
A wine most dear to me.
Angora goat's-milk cheese, though fare
Fit for the gods, can scarce compare,
Anitra, ah, with thee!
(*Hangs his lute over his shoulder and goes nearer
the tent.*)
Silence! Is my fair one listening?
Did she hear my little song?
Is she peeping through the curtain,
Veils etcetera cast aside?
[Hush! A sound! As of a cork
From a bottle gaily springing!
Now again! And yet again!
Sighs of passion? Love's sweet song?
No, it is the sound of snoring.
Heavenly sound! Anitra sleeps!
Nightingale, O cease thy scraping.
Woe and misery befall thee
If thou darest with gulp and gurgle—
Oh well, never mind, forget it.
Nightingale, thou art a singer.
Even such a one as I.
You, like me, bewitch with music
Gentle, tender, youthful hearts.
The cool night was made for music.
Music is our common sphere.

Music makes us what we are;
Peer Gynt and the nightingale.
And the fact that she lies sleeping
Makes my passion's bliss complete.
I poise my lips above the beaker,
The rich wine as yet untasted.]
No, bless my soul, here she comes.
[Well, after all, perhaps it's best.]

ANITRA (*from within the tent*). Dost thou call in the
night, O Master?

PEER. I do indeed. The Prophet calls.
I was wakened by the cat
Uttering violent hunting-cries.

ANITRA. Oh, Master, those weren't hunting-cries.
[They were something much worse.]

PEER. What?

ANITRA. I dare not tell thee.

PEER. Speak!

ANITRA. I blush—

PEER (*comes closer*). The same passion that inspired me
When I gave you my great opal?

ANITRA (*horrified*). O treasure of the world, dost thou
liken thyself to an old tom-cat?

PEER. Child, torn by love tom-cats and prophets
Behave very much the same.

ANITRA. Jests flow like honey from thy lips, O Master.

PEER. My little friend, [you must not judge
Great men by their exteriors.]
I am at heart a jovial man,
Especially in private audience.
[I am bound by my position
To assume a solemn mask.
Daily duties cramp my style.
My numerous worries and anxieties
Make me sometimes rather surly.
But that's just my way of speaking.

Away with all that! *En tête-à-tête*
I'm Peer—I mean—well, whoever I am.]
Come on, let's forget the Prophet.
Here you see me as myself.
    (*Sits under a tree and pulls her over to him.*)
[Come, Anitra, we will rest
Beneath the palm-tree's gentle fan.
I shall whisper, you shall smile.
Then we'll change parts, and your sweet lips
Will whisper love and make me smile.]

ANITRA (*lies down at his feet*). All thy words are sweet
    as song,
  Though I understand little. Tell me, Master,
  Can thy daughter get a soul by listening?

PEER. Soul, knowledge, spiritual enlightenment—
  You shall have them
  When in the East, on rosy streamers,
  Letters of fire proclaim the day.
  Then, my child, I'll give you lessons.
  [You'll get your education.]
  But now, in the night's sweet stillness,
  Why should I act the schoolmaster
  [With the threadbare remnants of my wisdom]?
  The soul is not the most important thing.
  The heart is what counts.

ANITRA. Speak, O Master. When thou speakest
  I see a glimmer, as of opals.

PEER. Too much wisdom leads to folly.
  [The bud of cowardice, forced to fullest bloom,
  Swells into tyranny. Truth pushed to excess
  Reads like a wise text written backwards.
  Yes, my daughter, this world is full of people
  So spiritually gorged that their eyes are blinded.
  I knew such a fellow once, a pearl among men,
  But he came to nothing, losing all sense in sound.
  Do you see the desert surrounding this oasis?
  Simply by flicking this turban, I could conjure
  The seas of the world in to flood every acre.

But to create new lands and seas would be
Sheer madness.] Do you know the secret of life?

ANITRA.   No, tell me.

PEER.   [It is to float dry-shod down the river of time;]
To be oneself.
Only in the vigour of youth
Can I be myself, my child.
Age makes eagles lose their feathers,
Age makes old men shake and pine.
[Age makes women bald and toothless,]
Age gives misers withered hands.
Age shrinks hearts and withers souls.
Youth, ah! Youth! I shall rule
Like a Sultan, hot and strong!
Not on the shores of Gyntiana
Underneath the palms and vines,
But in the fresh and waving pastures
Of a maiden's virgin thoughts.
[So you see, my little girl, why
I have condescended to seduce you;
Why I chose your little heart
For my empire.
I shall rule your every longing,
Tyrant in my state of love!
You shall live for me alone.
I shall possess you, like a jewel.
Should we part, then life will cease—
That is, yours. So kindly note that.
Every inch and fibre of you
Must accept me as its master.
You shall have no will but mine.]
The midnight beauties of your hair,
All your rich loveliness, shall draw me
Like the Babylonian Gardens
To my royal trysting-place.
[So it's best your head is empty.
If one has a soul, one wastes so much time
In introspection. And while we're on the subject,

You can have a chain around your ankle.
Then we'll both be happy.]
My soul will do for both of us.
[In other respects, we'll maintain the *status quo*.]
                    (ANITRA *snores*.)
What? She's asleep! Has everything I've said
Been thrown away? No, that's another sign
Of my power. My talk of love bears her away
Like a river into dreamland.
           (*Gets up and puts jewels in her lap*.)
Here are jewels! And here are more!
Sleep, Anitra! Dream of Peer!
Sleep. By sleeping you have set
The crown on my imperial brow.
Tonight, by force of personality,
Peer Gynt has won his victory.

———————

*A caravan route. The oasis is visible far away in the
background.* PEER GYNT, *on his white horse, is riding furi-
ously through the desert with* ANITRA *in front of him on
his saddle-bow*.

ANITRA. Let me go! I'll bite you!

PEER. You little rogue!

ANITRA. What do you want?

PEER. What do I want? To play at hawk and dove.
  To carry you off! To play mad games with you!

ANITRA. Shame on you! An old prophet—!

PEER. Oh, rubbish. The Prophet isn't old, you little
     goose.
  Do you think this is a sign of age?

ANITRA. Let me go! I want to go home!

PEER. Now you're being a coquette.
  Home? To Daddy? A fine idea!
  [We're two wild birds that have flown from our cage,]
  We never dare enter his sight again.

Besides, [my dear, one should never stay too long
In the same place. The better people know you,
The less they respect you. Especially when you're a
    prophet
Or anything like that. One should come and go
Fleetingly, like a vision;] it was time I moved on.
[They're fickle fellows, these sons of the sand.]
I was getting no incense or prayers in the end.

ANITRA. But are you a Prophet?

PEER. I am your Emperor! (*Tries to kiss her.*)
    My little woodpecker's being coy.

ANITRA. Give me that ring you've got on your finger.

PEER. Anitra, my dearest, take all I have.

ANITRA. Your words are music. [They bewitch me.]

PEER. It's wonderful to know that you love me so dearly.
    [I'll dismount, and lead your horse like a slave.
        (*Hands her the whip and dismounts.*)
    There now, my rose, my fairest flower.
    I'll trudge beside you through the sand
    Till I'm hit by sunstroke and meet my end.]
    I'm young, Anitra! Remember that.
    [So don't be alarmed if I seem to be frivolous.
    A sense of fun is inseparable from youth.
    If you had a few more brains in your head,
    My sweet little lily, you'd understand
    My playfulness is proof that I am young.]

ANITRA. Yes, you're young. Have you any more rings?

PEER. [Of course I am!] Catch! I can jump like a stag!
    If we had vine-leaves, I'd garland myself.
    Yes, of course I am young! Yoo-hoo! I'm going to dance!
        (*Dances and sings.*)
    I'm a happy little cock!
    Come and peck me, little hen!
    Yoo! Hup! Trippety-trip!
    I'm a happy little cock!

ANITRA. You're sweating, Prophet. I'm afraid you'll melt.
    Give me that heavy thing on your belt.

PEER.   O tender care! Carry my purse for ever!
    [Hearts that love are happy without gold.
                    (*Dances and sings again.*)
    Young Peer Gynt is a naughty madcap.
    He doesn't know his tummy from his toes.
    "Pish!" says Peer, "Pish! Anything goes!"
    Young Peer Gynt is a naughty madcap.

ANITRA.   How exalting to see the Prophet dance!

PEER.   Never mind the Prophet.] Let's change clothes!
    Yoo-hoo! Take them off!

ANITRA.   Your cloak would be too long, your belt too
        wide,
    And your stockings too tight.

PEER (*kneels*).   Then inflict some ordeal on me!
    To a heart full of love, it is sweet to suffer.
    Listen. As soon as we get to my castle—

ANITRA.   In Paradise. Have we far to ride?

PEER.   O, a thousand miles!

ANITRA.   Too far!

PEER.   O listen! You shall have the soul I promised you—

ANITRA.   Thanks, I'll manage without a soul.
    But you asked for an ordeal—

PEER (*gets up*).   Yes, by Allah! Let it be short, but hard!
    A moment of exquisite pain!

ANITRA.   Anitra obeys the Prophet! Farewell!
    (*She hits him sharply across the fingers and gallops
                back across the desert.*)

PEER (*stands for a long while as though thunderstruck*).
        Well, I'll be—!

    ―――――――――

*The same, an hour later. PEER GYNT, soberly and re-
flectively, is removing his Turkish costume, garment by
garment. Finally he takes his little travelling-cap out of
the pocket of his coat, puts it on, and stands once again
in European dress.*

PEER (*throws the turban far away*). There lies the
Turk and here stand I!
[This heathen life won't do at all.
Thank goodness I only borrowed clothes
And wasn't born to it. *Mon Dieu, mon Dieu,
Qu'allais-je faire dans cette galère?*][19]
It's best, after all, to live as a Christian.
[To put behind one all peacock pretensions
And steer one's course by law and morality.
To be oneself and get at the end
A speech by the graveside and flowers on one's coffin.]
(*Walks a few paces.*)
That bitch. She was within an ace of turning my head.
[I'm damned if I'll ever understand
What it was that bemused me. Well, thank heavens
it's over.]
I nearly made a fool of myself.
[It's lucky that joke was carried no further.
I have erred. That's true. But it wasn't my fault.
I was simply placed in a false situation.
It wasn't I myself who fell from grace.
This prophetic life is divorced from reality
And took its revenge with this show of bad taste.
It's a rotten profession, this being a prophet.
Its nature demands that you live in a mist.
As soon as you behave like a rational being
You're finished. I was only acting professionally
In pretending I was in love with that little goose.
All the same—
(*Bursts into laughter.*)
Just fancy!
Trying to make time stop by dancing!
Trying to swim against the current
By fluttering my feathers and wagging my tail!
Playing on the lute, and caressing and sighing,
And ending by getting properly plucked!
Such conduct is truly prophetic madness.
Plucked! Yes, she's certainly plucked me clean.
Still, I have a little left here in my pocket;

And a bit more hidden away in America.]
I'm not a beggar yet. And maybe this halfway house
Is best; to be neither rich nor poor.
I'm not dependent on coachman or horses,
And don't need to bother with trunks or carriage.
In short, I am master of the situation,
As the saying is. Which path shall I choose?
Many lie open. [And it's the choice
That distinguishes the wise man from the fool.
My business life is a finished chapter.
My love-life is a cast-off shirt.]
I don't feel inclined to retreat like a crab.
"Forward or back, it's equally far.
Outside or in, I'm still confined."
That's how it stands in some clever book,
[I think. Something new, then. Something noble.
A goal that's worth my money and labour.]
Suppose I wrote my autobiography?
[Candidly, to show people the way
And give them a lead to imitate?]
No, wait! [I've plenty of time on my hands.]
I might become a wandering scholar
And study the decline of man.
[Yes, that is the road for me!
I loved stories when I was a child.
And I've read a good deal of them since.] Yes, that's it!
I'll trace the path of the human race,
Float like a feather on the stream of time,
Re-live man's history, as in a dream;
See the great heroes wage their battles for truth
(As a spectator, from a safe distance);
I'll see thinkers perish, and martyrs bleed,
Empires founded and empires fall,
Mighty epochs growing from small beginnings—
In short, I shall skim the cream of history.
[I must try to get hold of a copy of Becker[20]
And arrange my travels chronologically.
Admittedly my knowledge isn't very thorough,
And the inner machinery of history is complicated—

But what of that? Original conclusions
Are often reached from the most unlikely starting-
      point.]
How fine to set oneself a goal
And drive one's way remorselessly towards it!
                    (*Quiet, moved.*)
To sever the bonds that bind one to one's [home
And] friends. To say farewell to earthly riches,
And bid the sweet joys of love goodnight,
All to seek out the mystery of truth.
                    (*Wipes a tear from his eye.*)
That is the test of the true scientist.
Oh, I feel so happy!
Now I have fathomed the riddle of my destiny
[And shall struggle towards it, however hard the road].
It is surely pardonable to feel a little proud;
And know that I am myself, Peer Gynt,
[Also called] Emperor of the Life of Man.
I shall hold the whole of the past in my hands.
I'll never more tread in the paths of the living.
The present is worthless. Man has no faith nor courage.
His soul is earthbound, his actions meaningless.
                    (*Shrugs his shoulders.*)
And as for women—they're not worth one's breath.
                    (*Goes.*)

---

*A summer day, far up in the North. A forest hut; the
open door has a large wooden bar on it. Reindeer's antlers
over the door. A flock of goats is grazing by the wall of
the hut.* SOLVEIG, *now a middle-aged woman, but still
fair-haired and beautiful, is sitting outside in the sunshine,
spinning.*

SOLVEIG (*looks down the path and sings*). Winter may
      pass, and spring,
And summer too, and the whole long year.
But some time I know that you will come,

And I shall wait, as I promised I would
[When I saw you last, my dear.]
(*Calls the goats, then turns back to her spinning
                    and singing.*)
God give you strength, wherever you may be.
God give you joy, if you stand before his footstool.
I shall wait here till you come back to me.
                    (*Looks upwards.*)
And if it's there you're waiting, we shall meet there, my
     friend.

---

*In Egypt. Dawn. The statue of Memnon[21] stands in
the sand.* PEER GYNT *enters on foot and glances briefly
around.*

PEER.   The statue of Memnon.
This would be a good place to start my travels.
Now I'll become an Egyptian for a change.
[But firmly based upon the Gyntian self.
Afterwards I'll move on to Assyria.]
I don't need to begin at Genesis.
I'll go round all that Biblical stuff.
[I'll probably come across the odd relic of it,
But to investigate its seams, as the saying goes,]
That's outside my plan. [It would overtax my strength.]
                    (*Sits on a stone.*)
Now I shall rest and wait patiently
Till the Statue has sung its usual morning song.
After breakfast I'll climb up the Pyramid,
And glance inside it, if I have time.
Then I'll journey by land round the Red Sea.
I might find King Potiphar's grave.
Then I'll turn Asiatic! In Babylon
I'll look for the Hanging Gardens and the Concubines—
Hm—I mean the chief traces of ancient culture.
Then straight on to the walls of Troy.
From Troy I can voyage directly by sea

To great old Athens. [And there, on the very spot,
I'll look at the pass Leonidas defended.
I'll acquaint myself with the better philosophers,
And find the prison where Socrates sacrificed
His life. Oh, no, I forgot—there's a war on there.
Well, my Hellenic phase will have to wait.]
                    (*Looks at his watch.*)
It's too bad, how long one has to sit around
Before the sun rises. My time is short.
Well, after Troy—that was where I'd got to—
                    (*Gets up and listens.*)
What's that curious whispering sound?

                    (*Sunrise.*)

MEMNON STATUE (*sings*). From the demi-god's ashes
        there rise, youth-renewing,
Birds ever singing.
Zeus the All-Knowing
Shaped them for battle.
O Owl of Wisdom, where do my birds sleep?
You must solve the riddle of my song or die.

PEER.   How strange! I really thought a sound
Came from the Statue. The music of the past!
I heard a voice like stone rising and falling.
I must note that.
                    (*Writes in his notebook.*)
"The Statue sang. I heard the sound clearly,
But did not quite understand the words.
The whole thing was of course a hallucination,
Saw nothing else of interest today."
                    (*He goes on.*)

_____

*Near the village of Gizeh. The Great Sphinx carved out
of the rock. In the distance can be glimpsed the spires and
minarets of* Cairo. PEER GYNT *enters and studies the
Sphinx closely, now through his lorgnette, now through his
hollowed hand.*

PEER. The Great Sphinx of Gizeh. Now where in the
    world
Have I met before something like this monster?
Something I've half forgotten. [I've met it
Somewhere.] Was it a man? And if so, who?
That statue, Memnon, it struck me later,
Looked like [that character in the fairy books,
The one they call] the Old Man of the Mountains.
[Squatting up there, so stiff and still,
With a couple of columns supporting his rump.]
But this extraordinary mongrel,
This changeling, half woman and half lion,
Did I read about it in a story book too?
Or did I actually meet it somewhere?
[A story book?] Ah yes, now I remember.
[Of course!] It's the Boyg, that I hit on the head—
I mean, I dreamed I did. I was running a fever—
               (*Goes closer.*)
The same eyes. And the selfsame lips.
Not quite so torpid. And a little more cunning.
But otherwise pretty much the same.
Hullo, old Boyg. So you look like a lion
When viewed from behind in the daylight.
Do you still talk riddles? We'll try.
Let's see if you answer the same as before.
          (*Shouts at the Sphinx.*)
Hi, Boyg! Who are you?

A VOICE (*from behind the Sphinx*). *Ach, Sfinx, wer bist
    du?*

PEER. What was that? An echo in German? How
    strange!

VOICE. *Wer bist du?*

PEER. It speaks the language fluently.
This observation is new, and mine.
           (*Writes in his notebook.*)
"Echo in German. Dialect: Berlin."
    (BEGRIFFENFELDT *emerges from behind the Sphinx.*)

BEGRIFFENFELDT. A man!

PEER. [Oh, it was him talking.] (*Writes again.*)
"Later came to another conclusion."

BEGRIFFENFELDT (*making all kinds of restless gestures*).
Excuse me, *mein Herr. Eine lebensfrage—*
What makes you come here on this particular day?

PEER. I'm just visiting an old friend of my youth.

BEGRIFFENFELDT. What? The Sphinx—?

PEER (*nods*). Yes. I used to know him well when I was
younger.

BEGRIFFENFELDT. *Wunderbar!* After such a night!
My head is throbbing. It is ready to burst.
You know him, man? Speak! Answer!
Can you tell me who he is?

PEER. Who he is? That's easy enough. He is *himself*.

BEGRIFFENFELDT (*gives a jump*). Ha! In a flash, the
answer to life's riddle!
You are sure he is himself?

PEER. Yes. Well, he says so, anyway.

BEGRIFFENFELDT. Himself! Then the hour of revolution
is at hand!
(*Takes off his hat.*)
Your name, *mein Herr?*

PEER. I was christened Peer Gynt.

BEGRIFFENFELDT (*in hushed admiration*). Peer Gynt!
Allegorical! I might have expected it!
Peer Gynt! That means The Unknown.
The Messiah whose coming was revealed to me—

PEER. No, really? You've come here to meet—?

BEGRIFFENFELDT. Peer Gynt! What profundity! What
mystery! What penetration!
Each word is like the voice of infinity!
What are you?

PEER (*modestly*). I have always tried to be myself.
Here is my passport.

BEGRIFFENFELDT. That enigmatic word again!
(*Seizes him by the wrist.*)   To Cairo.

The Emperor of Interpreters is found!

PEER. Emperor?

BEGRIFFENFELDT. Come!

PEER. People know of me—?

BEGRIFFENFELDT (*drags him away*). The Emperor of Interpreters! The Prophet of Self!

———————————

In Cairo. A big courtyard surrounded by high walls and buildings. Barred windows. Iron cages. THREE WARDERS *in the courtyard.* A FOURTH WARDER *enters.*

FOURTH WARDER. Hi, Schafmann, where's the director?

ANOTHER WARDER. He went out this morning before daybreak.

FOURTH WARDER. I think something must have annoyed him.
Last night he—

OTHER WARDER. Hush! There he is!
(BEGRIFFENFELDT *enters, leading* PEER GYNT. *He locks the gate and pockets the key.*)

PEER (*to himself*). This is a very clever man.
I can hardly understand a word he says.
                    (*Looks round.*)
So this is the Philosophers' Club you spoke of?

BEGRIFFENFELDT. Yes, here they are, every man of them.
The Circle of the Seventy Interpreters;[22]
Recently increased by a hundred and sixty.
                    (*Shouts at the* WARDERS.)
Mikkel, Schlingelberg, Schafmann, Fuchs!
Get into your cages at once!

WARDERS. Us?

BEGRIFFENFELDT. Who else? Get in, get in!
When the world turns over, we must do the same.
                    (*Forces them into a cage.*)
He's arrived this morning—the mighty Peer!

You can guess the rest, I need say no more.
(*Locks the cage and throws the key into a well.*)

PEER.   But, my dear Doctor—director—

BEGRIFFENFELDT.   Neither. I used to be—! Herr Peer,
Can you keep a secret? I must tell someone—

PEER (*increasingly uneasy*).   What is it?

BEGRIFFENFELDT.   Promise you won't get frightened?

PEER.   I'll try—

BEGRIFFENFELDT (*drags him into a corner and whispers*).
Absolute Reason passed away at eleven o'clock last
night.

PEER.   God help me—!

BEGRIFFENFELDT.   Yes, it's a terrible tragedy.
And especially unpleasant for me, in my position.
Up to now, this institution
Has been regarded as a madhouse.

PEER.   A madhouse?

BEGRIFFENFELDT.   Not now, you understand.

PEER (*pale, whispers*).   Yes, I understand!
This man is mad, and no one knows it.
(*He edges away.*)

BEGRIFFENFELDT (*follows him*).   I hope you don't mis-
understand me?
When I say he is dead, that isn't strictly true.
He's beside himself. Jumped out of his skin.
[Just like my compatriot Munchausen's fox.][23]

PEER.   Excuse me a minute—

BEGRIFFENFELDT (*holds him back*).   [No, not like a fox.]
Like an eel.
A needle through his eye, and he was squiggling on the
wall—

PEER.   How am I going to get out—?

BEGRIFFENFELDT.   A razor round his neck, and pip! —out
of his skin!

PEER.   He's mad! A raving lunatic!

BEGRIFFENFELDT. Now it's obvious that if Reason has
     jumped out of his skin,
That must mean a complete revolution all over the
     world.
Those persons who were formerly regarded as mad
Became sane at eleven o'clock last night
[In accordance with this new phase of Reason].
Moreover, if one considers logically,
It is clear that at the hour I mentioned
The so-called sane began to rave.

PEER. You mentioned the hour. My time is rather
     short—

BEGRIFFENFELDT. Your time? Of course! That reminds
     me.
                    (*Opens a door and shouts.*)
Come out, my children! The promised hour has come!
Reason is dead! Long live Peer Gynt!

PEER. Now, my dear fellow—
          (THE LUNATICS *wander out into the courtyard.*)

BEGRIFFENFELDT. Good morning! Come out here and
     greet the dawn
Of liberation. Your Emperor is here!

PEER. Emperor?

BEGRIFFENFELDT. Of course.

PEER. But the honour is too great. Really too much—

BEGRIFFENFELDT. Oh, this is no time for false modesty.

PEER. But at least give me time! No, I'm not worthy—
     I am stupefied—

BEGRIFFENFELDT. A man who has solved the riddle of
     the Sphinx?
A man who is himself!

PEER. That's just it. I *am* myself in everything.
But here, as far as I can make out,
The thing is to be beside oneself.

BEGRIFFENFELDT. Beside oneself? No, there you're quite
     mistaken.
Here we are ourselves with a vengeance;
Ourselves and nothing whatever but ourselves.

[We go full steam through life under the pressure of
    self.]
Each one shuts himself up in the cask of self,
Sinks to the bottom by self-fermentation,
Seals himself in with the bung of self,
And seasons in the well of self.
No one here weeps for the woes of others.
No one here listens to anyone else's ideas.
We are ourselves, in thought and in deed,
Ourselves to the very limit of life's springboard.
So, if we are to have an Emperor,
It's obvious that you are just the man.

PEER. Oh, if only—!

BEGRIFFENFELDT. Don't be depressed. Everything seems
    new at first.
"Oneself." Come here, you shall see an example.
We'll choose the first that comes. (*To a melancholy
    figure.*)
Good morning, Huhu.[24] Well, my boy,
Still wandering round so miserably?

HUHU. What else can I do when race after race
    Dies uninterpreted?
                    (*To* PEER.)
You're a stranger here. Will you listen to me?

PEER (*bows*). Certainly.

HUHU. Then lend me your ear.
    Far in the East, like garlands round a brow
    Lie the coasts of Malabar. [The Portuguese
    And Dutch have brought their culture to the land.]
    Many Malabaris still live there.
    But foreigners have messed the language up.
    And now they are masters of the land.
    But long ago, the orang-utang ruled.
    He was the forest's lord and master;
    [He was free to fight and to snarl in freedom]
    Grinning and gaping as Nature created him.
    He could fight and shriek in perfect freedom.
    [He was master in his own kingdom.]

But then, alas, the foreigners came
And stifled the original language of the jungle.
[For four whole centuries the simian race
Brooded in darkness. And, as is well known,
Such long nights leave their mark upon a people.]
Now the voice of the jungle is silenced.
Grunts and growls are heard no more.
Now we can only express our thoughts
Through the medium of speech. How intolerably
    cramping!
[Dutchmen and Portuguese, half-castes and Malabaris
Suffer equally.] I have fought to restore
Our native tongue, the primal speech of the jungle,
Tried to resuscitate its corpse;
Fought for our right to shriek and snarl;
Have shrieked and snarled myself; [and proved the need
For shrieks and snarls if our folk literature
Is to survive] but my work has not been appreciated.
Now perhaps you understand my sorrow.
Thank you for lending me your ear.
If you have advice, let me hear it.

PEER (*to himself*). "When surrounded by wolves it is
    best to howl."
    (*Aloud.*) My friend, I seem to remember that in
    Morocco
There live orang-utangs with no interpreter
[Or poet to speak for them]. Their language sounds
Like Malabari. Why don't you, like many great men,
Emigrate to serve your race?

HUHU. Thank you for your kind attention.
I will follow your advice.
        (*Waves an arm impressively.*)
East, thou hast disowned thy singer.
Apes shall flourish in the West.
        (*Goes.*)

BEGRIFFENFELDT. Well, wasn't he himself? I should have
    thought so.
[He's full of his ego; he has no room for anything else.
He is himself in everything he says

And does. Himself, because he is beside himself.)
Come here! Now I'll show you another one
Who since last night has been equally reasonable.
  (*To a* FELLAH[25] *bearing a mummy on his back.*)
King Apis! How goes it, mighty Lord?

FELLAH (*wildly, to* PEER).   Am I King Apis?

PEER (*edges behind* BEGRIFFENFELDT).   I must admit
    I'm afraid I'm not fully acquainted
With the situation. But, to judge from your tone,
I should imagine—

FELLAH.   Now you're lying, too.

BEGRIFFENFELDT.   Your Majesty must explain to this
    gentleman.

FELLAH.   Yes. I'll tell him my story.
                     (*Turns to* PEER GYNT.)
You see this man upon my back?
King Apis was his name.
But now he's just a mummy.
He's dead, for all his fame.

He sculpted the Great Sphinx, and built
The mighty Pyramid;
He fought the Roman and the Turk,
And brought them low, he did.

And therefore the Egyptians
Worshipped him as divine,
And fed with sacrifices
The Bull God in his shrine.

But I am this King Apis.
It is as clear as noon.
If you don't understand me now,
You'll understand me soon.

King Apis while out hunting
Was taken short, poor man,
So squatted for a minute
On my ancestor's land.

Now the earth King Apis fertilised
Nourished *me* with its corn.
And if further proof were needed,
I have invisible horns.

So isn't it a scandal
That no one calls me King?
Though I was born an Apis,
I'm just a paltry thing.

Oh sir, can't you advise me?
Help me resolve my fate;
And make these damned fools realise
I *am* King Apis the Great!

PEER. Your Majesty must build a larger Sphinx
And better Pyramids.

FELLAH. Well, that's a fine suggestion!
A fellah! A starving louse!
I haven't got the strength to keep
The rats out of my house.

Quick, think of something better.
Now tell me what I lack.
What is it that will make me like
King Apis on my back?

PEER. How if Your Majesty hanged yourself?
Wound in a shroud so grim,
And hidden in the earth's dark womb,
You'd start to look like him.

FELLAH. I'll do it! Where's a rope?
The gallows'll settle the doubt.
We won't look quite alike at first,
But time will smooth that out.
        (*Goes off and prepares to hang himself.*)

BEGRIFFENFELDT. Well, there's a real personality for
        you!
A man of method—

PEER. Yes, yes, I see.

But he's really hanged himself! My God!
I'm feeling dizzy! I'm going out of my mind—!

BEGRIFFENFELDT. A transitional state. It'll soon pass.

PEER. Transitional? To what?
Excuse me, I must be going—

BEGRIFFENFELDT (*holds him*). Are you mad?

PEER. Not yet. Mad? God forbid!
(*A commotion.* HUSSEIN, *a cabinet minister, forces his
way through the crowd.*)

HUSSEIN. They tell me an Emperor has arrived today.
(*To* PEER.)
Is it you?

PEER (*desperately*). Apparently.

HUSSEIN. Good! Then you must have notes to be answered?

PEER (*tears his hair*). All right! Why not? The madder
the better!

HUSSEIN. Will you do me the honour of dipping me?
(*Bows low.*)
I am a pen.

PEER (*bows even lower*). And I am a piece of scrawled
imperial parchment.

HUSSEIN. My story, Your Majesty, is briefly this.
People think I'm blotting paper. But I'm not. I'm a pen.

PEER. My story, Imperial Pen, is equally brief.
I'm a blank sheet of paper that no one will write on.

HUSSEIN. Nobody understands where my talent lies.
They all want to use me to soak up ink.

PEER. I was a book with a silver clasp, that a girl
Held in her hands. Whether we're called mad or sane,
It is merely a printer's error.

HUSSEIN. Can you imagine a more frustrating life
Than to be a pen, and never taste the edge of a knife?

PEER (*jumps high in the air*). Imagine being a reindeer!
To jump down from a height!

Falling and falling, and never to feel the ground under
  your hoof!

HUSSEIN. A knife! I am blunt! Come, cut me, slit me!
  The world will perish if someone doesn't sharpen me!

PEER. Alas for the world, which our Lord thought so
  good!

BEGRIFFENFELDT. Here is a knife.

HUSSEIN (*seizes it*). Ah, how I shall lick up the ink!
  What relief to cut oneself to a point!
                    (*Cuts his throat.*)

BEGRIFFENFELDT (*moves to one side*). Don't splash me.

PEER (*in increasing horror*). Hold him!

HUSSEIN. Hold me! Yes, that's the word! Hold me! Hold
  the pen!
  Put paper on the desk—!
                    (*Falls.*)
  I'm worn out! My postscript—! Don't forget it!
  He lived and he died a pen guided by other hands!

PEER (*becomes dizzy*). What shall I—? What am I? O
  Great One! Hold me safe!
  I'm whatever you wish! I'm a Turk, a sinner,
  A troll! Only help me! Something has burst!
                    (*Screams.*)
  I can't remember Your name!
  O help me, Thou, O Guardian of all madmen!
                    (*Sinks unconscious to the ground.*)

BEGRIFFENFELDT (*with a crown of straw in his hand,
  jumps and sits astride him*). [Ha! See him sitting
  enthroned in the mire!
  Beside himself!] Crown him now!
    (*Forces the crown on to his head and cries.*)
  Hail, Emperor! Hail Emperor of Self!

[SCHAFMANN (*from his cage*). Es lebe hoch der grosse
  Peer!]

ACT FIVE

On board a ship in the North Sea, off the Norwegian coast. Sunset. Stormy weather. PEER GYNT, *a vigorous old man with grizzled hair and beard, is standing aft on the poop. He is dressed partly in sailor's clothes, with a sea-man's jacket and long boots. His clothes are somewhat worn, and bear the marks of hard use. He himself is weather-beaten, and his face has grown harder.*

The CAPTAIN *of the ship is at the wheel beside the* STEERSMAN. *The crew are forward.*

PEER (*leans his arms on the gunwale and gazes landward*).
There's Hallingskarv in his winter fur;
An old man pluming himself in the evening sun.
Joekel, his brother, stands behind him,
Hooded still in his ice-green cloak.
Folgefaan lies so delicate,
Like a virgin in her white linen.
It's no use trying to turn your heads.
You'll never touch her, you old men of stone.

CAPTAIN (*shouts forward*). Another hand to the wheel, and hoist the lantern!

PEER. She's blowing up hard.

CAPTAIN. We'll have a storm tonight.

PEER. Can you see the Ronde from the sea?

CAPTAIN. No, of course not. It's hidden behind the snow-field.

PEER. And Blaahoe?

CAPTAIN. No. But in clear weather
If you go aloft you can see Galdhoepiggen.

PEER.   Where is Haarteig?

CAPTAIN (*points*).   Over there.

PEER.   Yes, of course.

CAPTAIN.   You seem to know these parts.

PEER.   When I sailed from Norway, I passed this way.
The dregs of memory stay in the glass.
        (*Spits and gazes towards the coast.*)
[Up there, where the clefts and scars are blue,
And the mountain valley is black and narrow
Like a ditch; and below, along the open fjords,
The people live.
                (*Looks at the* CAPTAIN.)
                In this country
They build their houses far apart.

CAPTAIN.   Yes, they're pretty scattered.]

PEER.   Will we be in by daybreak?

CAPTAIN.   Just about. If the night's not too bad.

PEER.   It's thickening in the west.

CAPTAIN.   It is.

PEER.   Remind me when I settle with you,
I'd like to give something to the crew.

[CAPTAIN.   Thank you.

PEER.   It won't be much. I made a bit
Over there, but I lost most of it.
Fate and I haven't quite hit it off.
You know what I've got on board.
Well, that's the lot. The rest—psst!

CAPTAIN.   It's enough to make you a big man here.

PEER.   I've no family.
There's no one awaiting this rich old bastard.
Well, at least I won't have to put up with any fuss on
        the quayside.

CAPTAIN.   Here comes the storm.

PEER.   Well, remember,
If any of your men are really short—
I'm not a man who looks closely at my money.]

CAPTAIN. That's generous of you. They're mostly poor
    men.
  They've all got wives and youngsters at home.
  [And their wages don't stretch far.]
  If they get a little extra, they'll not forget it.

PEER. What? Wives and children? Are they married?

CAPTAIN. Married? Yes, every man. [The cook's the
    poorest.
  There's always black hunger in his house.]

PEER. Married? Someone waiting to give them a good
    welcome?

CAPTAIN. Yes, as good as poor people can give.

PEER. When they come home, what'll happen?

CAPTAIN. Their wives'll give them a little extra some-
    thing
  For once—

PEER. A candle on the table?

CAPTAIN. Maybe two. And a dram—

PEER. And they sit there snugly round the hearth
  With their children around them? All talking at once,
  [No one lets anyone finish a sentence]
  They're so happy—?

CAPTAIN. That's about it. So they'll bless you for your
    promise—

PEER (bangs the gunwale with his fist). I'll be damned
    if I will! Do you think I'm mad?
  Why should I pay for other men's children?
  I've had to work hard to earn my money.
  There's no one waiting for old Peer Gynt.

CAPTAIN. Well, well, do as you please. It's your money.

PEER. Yes! It's mine!
  Give me my bill when we cast anchor.
  My fare as cabin passenger from Panama,
  And a tot of rum for the crew. That's all.
  [If I give any more you can knock me down the hatch-
    way.

CAPTAIN. It's my job as Captain to give you a receipt,
Not a thrashing.] Excuse me. The storm's coming on.
(*He goes forward. It has become dark. Lights are lit
in the cabin. The sea grows rougher. Thick mist and heavy
clouds.*)

PEER. [To have a home full of children; to be their joy.
To be always in the forefront of their minds.
To be followed on one's way by the thoughts of
others—]
There's no one who ever thinks of me.
Candles on the table! I'll put out those candles!
[I'll find some way!] I'll make them all drunk!
Not one of those fools shall go ashore sober.
They'll come home drunk to their wives and children.
They'll swear, and knock them about—all their love
destroyed!
[They'll frighten their loved ones out of their wits.
Their wives'll scream and run from the house,
Dragging their children with them. That will be
A joyful homecoming!]
      (*The ship heels violently. He staggers and has
            difficulty in keeping his balance.*)
                              That was a lurch!
The sea's still itself up here in the North!
[The old devil's working as though he'd been paid for it.
It's always the same up in these Northern waters.
They're sullen and churlish. Always trying to thwart
you.]

THE WATCH (*forward*). Wreck to windward!

CAPTAIN (*amidships*). Helm hard to starboard! Keep
her close to the wind!

STEERSMAN. Anyone on the wreck?

WATCH (*screams*). I can see three!

PEER. Quick! Lower a boat!

CAPTAIN. She'd fill before we cast off. (*Goes forward.*)

PEER. Who cares about that?
                  (*To some of the* CREW.)
                              If you're men, save them!
You're not afraid of getting wet, are you?

BOATSWAIN. It's impossible in a sea like this.

PEER. They're screaming again. Look, there's a lull!
You, cook! Will you try? I'll give you money!

COOK. Not if you gave me twenty pounds.

PEER. You dogs! You cowards! Don't you realise
These men have wives and children at home?
They are sitting, waiting for them—!

BOATSWAIN. Well, there's virtue in patience.

CAPTAIN. Bring her about!

STEERSMAN. The wreck's turned over.

PEER. How silent it is, suddenly!

BOATSWAIN. If they were married
This world's the richer by three new widows.
                (*The storm grows.* PEER GYNT *goes aft.*)

PEER. There's no faith left among men any more.
[Christianity's only preached and written;
There's little charity and less prayer.]
They've no respect for the powers above.
On a night like this our Lord is dangerous.
[These brutes should take care and remember
That it's dangerous to play with elephants.
They simply thumb their noses at Him.]
I'm guiltless. [On the Day of Judgment] I can swear
I stood ready and willing [with money in my hand].
But what good is that? [They say
An easy conscience makes the softest pillow.
That may be so on dry land, but at sea,
Where an honest man's like a fish out of water,
It's not the same.] A man can never be
Himself at sea. He must sink or swim with the rest.
If vengeance should strike the boatswain or the cook
I'll be sucked down to my death with the rest of them.
[One's individual virtues are ignored.
You're just a bit of meat for the sausage machine.]
My mistake is this. I've been too meek,
And I've had no thanks for it. If I were younger,
I'd change my style [and start acting the boss].

Well, there's still time. They shall learn in the parish
Peer Gynt has come riding back over the sea!
I'll get back our farm by hook or by crook.
I'll rebuild it. It shall shine like a palace.
But they won't be allowed to enter the door.
They shall stand at the gate and twiddle their caps;
They shall beg and grovel—that they can do—
But not one shall get a farthing out of me.
[I've had to cringe under the whip of Fate,
And they'll find that I, too, can wield the lash.]

THE STRANGE PASSENGER (*stands in the darkness at* PEER'S
    side and greets him amicably).   Good evening.

PEER.   Good evening. What—? Who are you?

STRANGE PASSENGER.   Your fellow passenger.

PEER.   I thought I was the only one.

STRANGE PASSENGER.   A mistaken impression, now cor-
    rected.

PEER.   But it's strange I should see you for the first time
    tonight.

STRANGE PASSENGER.   I never appear in the daytime.

PEER.   [Are you ill? You're as white as a sheet—

STRANGE PASSENGER.   Thank you, no. I am in excellent
    health.]

PEER.   What a storm!

STRANGE PASSENGER.   Yes! Beautiful!

PEER.   Beautiful?

STRANGE PASSENGER.   The waves are running as high as
    houses.
  It makes my mouth water. Think of the wrecks
  There will be tonight. Think of the corpses drifting
    ashore.

PEER.   God preserve us!

STRANGE PASSENGER.   Have you ever seen a man
    strangled?
  Or hanged—or drowned?

PEER.   What—!

STRANGE PASSENGER. They laugh; but their laughter is forced.

Most of them bite out their tongues.

PEER. Get away from me!

STRANGE PASSENGER. Just one question. Suppose we, for example,

Should strike on a rock, and sink in the darkness—

PEER. You think there is a danger—?

STRANGE PASSENGER. I don't really know what I ought to say.

But suppose, now, I should float and you should sink—

PEER. Oh, rubbish—!

STRANGE PASSENGER. It's just a hypothesis.

But when a man stands with one foot in the grave

He sometimes tends to be generous—

PEER (*puts his hand in his pocket*). Oh, money—

STRANGE PASSENGER. No, no. But if you would be so kind

As to bequeath me your valuable body—

PEER. What!

STRANGE PASSENGER. Only your corpse, you understand.

To help my researches—

PEER. Go away!

STRANGE PASSENGER. But, my dear sir, consider. It's to your advantage.

I'll open you up and let in the light.

I want to discover the source of your dreams.

I want to find out how you're put together—

PEER. Away!

STRANGE PASSENGER. But, my dear sir! A drowned body—!

PEER. Blasphemous man!

You're provoking the storm! Are you out of your mind?

Look at the sea! [These waves are like mountains!]

At any moment we may be killed.

[And you're acting as though you can hardly wait for it.]

STRANGE PASSENGER. I see you're not in a mood for dis-
    cussion.
  But time, they say, changes everything.
                    (*Nods amicably.*)
  We'll meet when you're sinking, if not before.
  Perhaps you'll be more in the humour then.
                    (*Goes into the cabin.*)

PEER.   Horrible fellows these scientists are!
  You damned freethinker!
                    (*To the* BOATSWAIN, *who is passing.*)
                            A word with you, friend.
  That passenger. What kind of a madman's he?

BOATSWAIN. I know of no passenger except yourself.

PEER.   No passenger—? [This gets worse and worse.]
                    (*To the* CABIN BOY, *who has just
                        come out of the cabin.*)
  Who went into the cabin just now?

CABIN BOY. The ship's dog, sir. (*Goes on past him.*)

WATCH (*shouts*). Land close ahead!

PEER.   My trunk! My strong-box! Get my things on
    deck!

BOATSWAIN. We've more important things to do.

PEER.   Captain—what I said just now—
  I was only joking. I'll help the cook—

CAPTAIN.   The jib's blown away!

STEERSMAN.   The foresail's gone!

BOATSWAIN (*shouts from forward*). Rocks under the
    bow!

CAPTAIN.   She'll go to pieces!
                    (*The ship strikes. Alarm and confusion.*)

———————

*Close off shore, among rocks and surf. The ship is sink-
ing. Through the mist can be glimpsed the dinghy, with
two men in it. A sea strikes it. It heels over, there is a*

scream, then for a few moments all is silent. Soon after-
wards the boat comes to the surface bottom upwards.
PEER GYNT'S *head appears close to it.*

PEER. Help! Help! A boat! Help! I'm drowning!
O Lord, save me! [That's what the Bible says—!]

COOK (*comes up on the other side of the boat*). O Lord
God! [For my children's sake!] Have mercy!
Let me reach the land! (*Seizes hold of the keel.*)

PEER. Let go!

COOK. Let go!

PEER. I'll hit you!

COOK. I'll hit you!

PEER. [I'll break your bones!] I'll kick you down!
[I'll hit you!] Let go! This boat won't take two!

COOK. No! Get off!

PEER. You get off!

COOK. No, no!

(*They fight. One of the* COOK'S *hands is disabled, but
he clings on with the other.*)

PEER. Off with that hand!

COOK. Spare me, sir! Think of my children at home!

PEER. I need my life more than you. I am still childless.

COOK. Let go! You've lived. I'm young.

PEER. Get on with it! Sink! You're dragging me down!

COOK. Have pity! For God's sake! No one will mourn
for you—!
(*His hand slips. He screams.*)
I'm drowning!

PEER (*grips him by the hair*). I'll hold you by the hair.
Say your prayers quickly.

COOK. I can't remember—everything's going dark—!

PEER. [Say whatever's most important.] Come on!

COOK. "Give us this day—"

PEER. [Never mind that, cook. You'll get all you need.

COOK. "Give us this day—"]

PEER. The same old song! It's clear what you were!
  (*The* COOK *slips from his grasp.*)

COOK (*sinking*). "Give us this day our—" (*Disappears.*)

PEER. Amen. You were yourself, to the very end.
 Ah, well.
   (*Draws himself up on to the keel.*)
     While there's life there's hope.

STRANGE PASSENGER (*catches hold of the boat*). Good
 morning.

PEER. Ugh!

STRANGE PASSENGER. I heard shouting. How nice to find
 you.
 Well, did I prophesy correctly?

PEER. Let go! Let go! It'll barely hold one!

STRANGE PASSENGER. I'm swimming with my left leg.
 I'll stay afloat
 If I can just hold on with my fingers
 [To this little splinter]. Now about that corpse of
 yours—

PEER. Shut up!

STRANGE PASSENGER. It's all you have left.

PEER. Be quiet!

STRANGE PASSENGER. Just as you please.
    (*Silence.*)

PEER. What are you doing?

STRANGE PASSENGER. [I'm being quiet.

PEER. Damn your tricks! What are you up to?]

STRANGE PASSENGER. Waiting.

PEER (*tears his hair*). I'm going mad. Who are you?

STRANGE PASSENGER (*nods*). A friend.

PEER. What else? Tell me!

STRANGE PASSENGER. What do you think? Do you know
 no one else like me?

PEER. The Devil—?

STRANGE PASSENGER (*softly*). Is it his way to light the
 lantern
On life's long pilgrimage of fear?

PEER. Ah! So you are a messenger of light?

STRANGE PASSENGER. My friend, have you even once a
 year
Known the true anguish of the soul?

PEER. Of course one's afraid, when danger threatens—
[But everything you say has another meaning.]

STRANGE PASSENGER. Yes, but have you once in life
Won the victory that only defeat can bring?

PEER (*looks at him*). If you have come to open a door
It was stupid not to come before.
What's the good of coming now
[When the sea's about to swallow me up]?

STRANGE PASSENGER. Would you have found that victory
In the [warmth and] comfort of your hearthside?

PEER. Perhaps not. But I thought you were joking.
[How could you think it would open my eyes?]

STRANGE PASSENGER. Where I come from, laughter is
 rated as high as tears.

[PEER. There's a time for everything. As the proverb says:
"The publican's meat is the bishop's poison."]

STRANGE PASSENGER. Those whose dust sleeps in funeral
 urns would tell you:
"The tragic mask is not for everyday wear."]

PEER. Get away! [You frighten me!] Leave me! [Go!]
I must get ashore! I will not die!

STRANGE PASSENGER. Oh, don't worry.
You won't die in the middle of the last act.
     (*Glides away.*)

PEER. [Well, at least I'm that much wiser.
God, what a boring moraliser!]

A churchyard high up in the mountains. A funeral is in progress. A PRIEST *and* VILLAGERS. *The last verse of a psalm is being sung.* PEER GYNT *comes past on the road outside.*

PEER (*at the gate*).   Here's one of my countrymen gone
      the way of all flesh.
Thank God it's not me.

PRIEST (*speaks at the graveside*).   Now, as his soul moves
      blindly towards its judgment
And his poor dust rests here, an empty husk,
Now, my dear friends, let me remind you
About this dead man's pilgrimage on earth.

    He was not wealthy, neither was he clever;
His bearing was unmanly, his voice was weak,
Uncertain in expressing an opinion.
[He scarce seemed master even in his home.
He slunk into church as though he sought to beg
Permission to take his place with all the rest.

    He came, as you all know, from Gudsbrandsdal,
And moved here when he was no more than a boy.]
And, you remember, till the day he died,
He always kept his right hand in his pocket.

    [That right hand in his pocket was the thing
That stamped his image sharply on our minds;
And this strange shyness, this embarrassment.
Where'er he went, he seemed to dread being seen.]
But though he chose to tread his path alone,
And lived and died a stranger in our midst,
Yet you all know, although he sought to hide it,
That hand we never saw bore but three fingers.

    I well recall one morning, years ago;
Recruiting officers had come to Lunde.
It was in time of war. [All mouths discussed
Our country's sufferings, and its likely fate.
I stood and watched. An old grey-headed Captain
Sat with the sergeants and the Burgomaster
Behind a table.] Lad after lad was measured,
Given his shilling, and sworn in as a soldier.

The room was full, and in the yard outside
The winter air was filled with young men's laughter.
  Then a name was called, and a new lad stepped in,
Pale as the snow that fringes a green glacier.
They called him closer. He faltered towards the table,
His right hand swathed in a bloodstained cloth.
He gasped and swallowed, trying to find words;
[But none would come, despite the Captain's questions]
Until at length, his thin young cheeks aflame,
[Now failing to find words, now gabbling fast]
He told some tale of an accident; a sickle had slipped
And cut off one of his fingers close to the stump.
  A silence filled the room.
Men looked at one another, and curled their lips,
Stoning his face with their dumb glances.
He felt their scorn although he did not see it.
Then the Captain, an old grey man, slowly rose.
He spat, pointed towards the door, and said: "Go!"
  And as he walked, men shrank on either side,
So that he ran the gauntlet through their midst.
He reached the door, and then took to his heels
Through woods, up hills and the high tumbling screes;
His home lay far away among the mountains.
  Some six months later he came to live among us
[With his mother, his betrothed and a new-born child].
He leased a patch of land up in the hills
Where the waste ground slopes upwards towards Lomb.
He married, built his house, broke the hard ground.
Success attended him, as many a proud
Acre bore witness, waving tall and gold.
[In church he kept his right hand in his pocket,
But in his home I warrant those seven fingers
Toiled fully as hard as any other man's eight.]
Then the spring floods swept everything away.
  [They saved nothing except their lives.] Naked
And poor, he cleared another patch of land.
Before the autumn came, fresh wood-smoke rose
From a homestead newly built in safer lee.

[Safer? From floods, but not from avalanche.]
Two years later it lay, crushed by the snow.
 But even the avalanche could not break his spirit.
He dug, raked, carted, cleared the strangled earth.
And, ere the next winter's snows had come,
For the third time his humble home arose.
 [Three sons he had, strong and intelligent lads.
They had to go to school, but it lay far off.
They had to go where the mountain path could not,
Across the scar, narrow and steepling.
What did he do? The eldest had to manage
Alone, as best he might; where the slope was steepest
His father roped him to himself, and hauled him,
Bearing the second in his arms, the youngest
Upon his back. So, year by year, he toiled.
His sons grew, flourished, and in time became men.
Now he might surely look for some reward.
But three rich gentlemen in the New World
Have forgotten their father in Norway, and the slow
  journeys to school.]
 His vision was narrow. Beyond the tiny circle
Of those who stood close to him, he saw nothing.
Those words that should have resounded in his heart
To him rang meaningless like tinkling cymbals.
[His race, his country, all we think great and glorious,
Were from his eyes veiled in perpetual mist.]
 But he was humble, humble was this man.
And from the day when the Captain rose, and spat,
And pointed, he carried his judgment on his brow,
[As surely as the brand of shame on his cheek]
And his three fingers hidden in his pocket.
A criminal in the eyes of the law? Perhaps.
But there is something that shines above the law
As surely as the highest mountain peak
Has clouds above it like yet loftier mountains.
This was no patriot. For Church and State
He was a barren tree. But on his mountainside,
In the narrow circle of home, where his work lay,
There he was great, because he was himself.

The metal of which God made him rang most true
Until the end. His life was as a lute
Whose strings are muted. Peace to thee, silent warrior,
Who strove and fell in thy small humble war.
    It is not for us to search the heart and reins.
That is no task for dust, but for its Maker.
But freely I hope and firmly I believe
This man is not a cripple in the eyes of God.

(*The* MOURNERS *disperse.* PEER GYNT *remains alone.*)

PEER.   [Now that's what I call Christianity.
There was nothing there that could distress anyone.
And the theme of the parson's sermon, that one must
        be
Inflexibly oneself, is edifying.]
                    (*Looks down into the grave.*)
Could this have been the lad who chopped off his
        finger
When I was felling wood that day in the forest?
Who knows? If I weren't standing here with my staff
By the graveside of this spiritual kinsman,
I could well believe it was I who lay here sleeping
And hearing, as in a vision, myself so praised.
[That's really a beautiful Christian custom
Charitably to reminisce
Over the life of the dear departed.]
I shouldn't mind accepting my judgment
At the hands of this good parish priest.
[Ah well, I've a few years yet before
The gravedigger comes and offers me lodging.
And as the Scripture says: "What's best is best,"
And: "Sufficient unto the day is the evil thereof,"
And: "Don't cross your bridges before you come to
        them."
Yes, the Church is the only true comforter.
I haven't fully appreciated it before.
But now I realise how good it is
To be assured by the voice of authority:
"As a man sows, so shall he reap."
One must be oneself and look after oneself

And one's own, in all things, whether great or small.
If your luck runs out, at least you've the honour
Of having lived your life in accordance with
The best principles.] Now home! Let the path
Be steep and narrow. Let Fate be spiteful to the end.
Yet old Peer Gynt will still go his own way
And remain, as always, poor but virtuous.
                    (*Goes.*)

---

*A hill with a dried river bed. A ruined mill stands on
the river bank. The ground is torn up, and has a waste
appearance. Higher up is a large farmhouse, where an
auction is taking place. A large crowd is gathered there.
There is drinking and much noise.* PEER GYNT *is sitting
on a heap of rubbish near the mill.*

PEER.   Forward or back, it's equally far.
    Outside or in, I'm still confined.
    [Time wears on, and so does the river.]
    Go round, said the Boyg. I must do that here.

MAN IN MOURNING.   There's only rubbish left now.
                    (*Catches sight of* PEER GYNT.)
    Have we strangers, too? God save you, friend.

PEER.   [Good day to you.] You're having a gay time.
    What is it, a christening or a wedding?

MAN IN MOURNING.   More rightly a housewarming.
    The bride's at home to a host of worms.

PEER.   And worms are fighting for what she's left.

MAN IN MOURNING.   The song is over; the story's done.

PEER.   Every story has the same ending,
    And every song is an old song.
    [I knew them all when I was a boy.]

A YOUTH OF TWENTY (*with a casting ladle*).   Look at
        what I've bought!
    This is the ladle Peer Gynt used
    To cast his silver buttons in!

ANOTHER YOUTH.   I've done better than that!
   Look! I've bought Peer Gynt's purse for a shilling!
[A THIRD.   Is that all?
   Only half a dollar for the pedlar's moneybags?]

PEER GYNT.   Peer Gynt? Who was he?

MAN IN MOURNING.   Cuckold to Death and to Aslak the
      smith.[26]

A MAN IN GREY.   You're forgetting me! Are you drunk?

MAN IN MOURNING.   You're forgetting the storehouse door
      at Heggstad.

[MAN IN GREY.   That's true. But you never used to be so
      particular—]

MAN IN MOURNING.   As long as she doesn't put horns on
      Death—

MAN IN GREY.   Come, cousin. A dram for kinship's sake.

MAN IN MOURNING.   What the hell do you mean, kin-
      ship? [You're drunk—]

MAN IN GREY.   [Oh, nonsense. Be blood ever so thin,]
   Everyone feels he's akin to Peer Gynt.
                  (Wanders off with him.)

PEER (softly).   One meets old friends.

A BOY (shouts after the MAN IN MOURNING).   Watch out,
      Aslak! If you get drunk
   My mother will rise from her grave and haunt you!

PEER (gets to his feet).   They say: "The deeper you dig,
      the better it smells."
   Not so here.

[A LAD (with a bearskin).   Look, the Cat of the Dovre![27]
      Or anyway his skin!
   It was he chased the trolls on Christmas Eve!]

ANOTHER LAD (with a reindeer's antlers).   Here's the
      buck that carried Peer Gynt
   Along the crest of the Gjendin Edge!

A THIRD (with a hammer, shouts to the MAN IN MOURN-
      ING).   Hi, Aslak, do you recognise this hammer?
   Was it this you used when the Devil split your walls?

A FOURTH (*his hands empty*). Mads Moen, here's the
    invisible cloak!
    The one Peer Gynt wore when he flew off with Ingrid!

PEER. Give me a drink, lads. I'm feeling old.
    I think I'll put up my own rubbish for auction.[28]

A LAD. What have you got?

PEER. A palace!
    It lies in the Ronde. It's got strong walls.

THE LAD. I'll bid you a button.

PEER. I'll take a dram.
    It'd be a sin to offer me less.

ANOTHER LAD. He's a funny old boy!
              (*People gather around him.*)

PEER (*shouts*). My charger, Grane! Who'll make me a
    bid?

ONE OF THE CROWD. Where is he?

PEER. Far away in the west!
    Towards the sunset, lads! That horse can fly
    As fast, as fast as Peer Gynt can lie!

VOICES. What else have you got?

PEER. I've gold and I've scrap.
    I bought them with ruin. I'll sell at a loss.

A LAD. Put them up!

PEER. A dream of a book with a silver clasp.
    You can have that for a placket.

THE LAD. Who wants dreams?

PEER. My Empire!
    I'll throw it among you. You can fight for it.

THE LAD. Do we get a crown too?

PEER. Of the finest straw.
    It'll fit the first man who puts it on.
    Wait a moment, here's more. A rotten egg.
    A madman's grey hairs. The Prophet's beard.
    I'll give them all to the one who can show me
    The signpost that says: "Here lies the way."

PARISH OFFICER (*enters*).   Look, if you go on like this
    you'll get arrested.

PEER (*hat in hand*).   Maybe. But, tell me, who was Peer
    Gynt?

PARISH OFFICER.   What—?

PEER.   Oh, please [Your Honour]! I beg you humbly—

PARISH OFFICER.   Well, they say he was a damned liar—

PEER.   A liar—?

PARISH OFFICER.   Yes. All the great deeds he'd ever heard
    of,
He pretended he'd done them. Well, excuse me,
I've other business— (*Goes.*)

PEER.   And where is he now, this remarkable man?

AN OLD MAN.   He went away [to some foreign land]
Across the sea. [Things went badly for him,
As one might have foreseen.] He was hanged many
    years ago.

PEER.   Hanged? Well, well! [I guessed as much].
Poor old Peer Gynt! He remained himself
To the very end.
              (*Bows.*)
Goodbye [and thank you, kind sirs].
        (*Goes a few steps, and then stops.*)
Well, my merry lads and lasses,
Shall I repay your kindness with a story?

SEVERAL.   Yes. Do you know any?

PEER.   Why, yes. I do.
(*Goes closer to them. A strange expression comes over
his face.*)
In San Francisco, once, I was digging for gold.
The whole city was filled with mountebanks.
One could play the violin with his toes.
Another danced the bolero on his knees.
[A third, they say, wrote poetry
While someone bored a hole into his brain.]
One day the Devil came and joined the circus.
[He thought he'd try his luck like all the others.]

His trick was being able to grunt like a pig.
His personality impressed them all,
Though no one recognised him.
[The house was full, and anticipation ran high.]
He stepped on to the stage in a big flowing cloak.
[*Man muss sich drappieren*, as the Germans say.]
What they didn't know was that under the cloak
He'd hidden a real pig. [At length the performance
        started.]
The Devil pinched, and the pig let out a squeal.
[People accepted it as a fantasia
On our porcine existence, with its combination
Of liberty and bondage.] Then it gave
A screech as though its throat had been cut,
At which he bowed his thanks and went.
The experts discussed the performance and dissected it.
[Some praised it, some condemned.]
Some found the tone of the squeals too thin.
Others thought the death-shriek a trifle affected.
But on one point all were agreed. The actual grunting
Had been, throughout, decidedly exaggerated.
So the Devil got his due; a just reward
For over-estimating the intelligence of his audience.
(*He bows and goes. An uncertain silence falls on the*
CROWD.)

Whitsun Eve. Inside the forest. Behind, in a clearing,
is a cabin, with reindeer antlers above the door. PEER
GYNT *is crawling in the undergrowth gathering wild*
onions.

PEER. Well, I've reached one resting-place. Where's the
        next?
One must try them all, and choose the best.
I've tried the lot. I started as Caesar
And I've come right down to Nebuchadnezzar.
[I've gone back to the Bible after all;
The old boy's had to crawl back to his mother.]

Well, [the Scripture says: "Of dust thou art made,"
And] the first thing in life is to fill one's belly.
Onions? That won't get me far.
I'll have to be cunning and lay some snares.
There's a river here, so I won't go thirsty.
[The beasts'll still regard me as their boss.]
When I have to die, as die I must,
I'll creep under a tree blown down by the wind.
I'll heap leaves all over me like a bear
And I'll carve on the bark in big bold letters:
"Here lies Peer Gynt. A decent chap,
Emperor? (*Chuckles.*) You old fake!
You're no Emperor. You're just an onion.
Now then, little Peer, I'm going to peel you,
And you won't escape by weeping or praying.
    (*Takes an onion and peels it layer by layer.*)
The outermost layer is withered and torn;
That's the shipwrecked man on the upturned keel.
Here, mean and thin, is the passenger;
But it still tastes a little of old Peer Gynt.
And inside that is the digger of gold;
Its juice is all gone, if it ever had any.
[Who's this coarse fellow with calloused skin?
Ah, he's the trapper from Hudson Bay.]
This next one's shaped like a crown. No, thank you!
We'll throw that away, and ask no questions.
Here's the student of history, short and tough;
And here is the Prophet, fresh and juicy;
[Like the man in the proverb] he stinks of lies
That would blind an honest man's eyes with tears.
This layer now that curls up so softly
Is the sybarite living for ease and pleasure.
The next one looks sick; it's streaked with black.
That might mean a priest; or it might mean a nigger.
                    (*Peels off several at once.*)
What a terrible lot of layers there are!
Surely I'll soon get down to the heart?
                    (*Pulls the whole onion to pieces.*)
No—there isn't one! Just a series of shells

All the way through, getting smaller and smaller!
Nature is witty!
                    (*Throws the pieces away.*)
[I'm thinking too much. If you start going round
With your head in the clouds, you fall flat on your face.
Well, that's a danger I needn't worry about.
I'm safe on all fours.
                    (*Scratches his head.*)
Life is a fox. When you think you've got her
She slips through your grasp, and you're left holding
Something different, or nothing at all.]
(*He has come close to the cabin. He sees it and
starts.*)
This hut? On the moor—!
                    (*Rubs his eyes.*)
I feel as though I'd seen it before.
Those antlers sprouting above the doorway—
[That mermaid, shaped like a fish from her navel—
It's a lie! There's no mermaid. Just nails and planks
To shut out nagging hobgoblin thoughts—]

SOLVEIG (*sings in the hut*).   The house is ready for Pen-
          tecost.
My love is far away.
Come back, come back to me.
If your burden is heavy,
Take your time.
I will wait for you, my love.

PEER (*gets to his feet silently, pale as death*).   One who
          remembered—and one who forgot.
One who kept what the other has lost.
And the game can never be played again!
Oh, here was my Empire and my crown!
                    (*Runs down the forest path.*)

———————

*Night. A moor, with pine trees. A forest fire has ravaged
it. Charred tree-trunks can be seen for miles around. Here
and there white mist patches hug the earth.* PEER GYNT
is running across the moor.

PEER. [Ashes, mist, and dust and wind!
  That's the stuff with which to build!
  Our palace shall be proud and fair
  As befits a sepulchre.

  Foolish dreams and stillborn wisdom
  Shall be our palace's foundation.
  Out of them it shall tower high.
  Every stone shall be a lie!

  Let fear of truth and of repentance
  Flame like fire upon the summit
  Sounding forth the trump of doom:
  Petrus Gyntus Caesar fecit!]

  What is this sound of children weeping?
  Weeping but halfway to song?
  Threadballs are rolling at my feet—
                  (*Kicks them.*)
  Get away! You're blocking my path!

THREADBALLS[29] (*on the ground*). We are thoughts.
  You should have thought us.
  You should have given us
  Little feet.

PEER (*goes round them*). I gave birth to one.
  It was a monster with a twisted leg.

THREADBALLS. We should have flown
  Like children's voices.
  Here we roll on the ground,
  Grey balls of thread.

PEER (*stumbles*). Thread! Rubbish!
  Would you trip your father? (*Flees.*)

WITHERED LEAVES (*flying before the wind*). We are a
      trumpet-call.
  You should have sounded us.
  See how your sloth
  Has shrunk and withered us.
  The worm has gnawed us

Through and through.
We never wound
Ourselves round fruit.

PEER. You weren't born in vain.
Lie still. You'll make good manure.

A WHISPERING IN THE AIR. We are songs.
You should have sung us.
A thousand times
You have stifled and strangled us.
In the mine of your heart
We have lain and waited.
We were never summoned.
Curse you! Curse you!

PEER. Curse you, fools!
Did I have time to make up verses?
                    (*Tries to take a short cut.*)

DEWDROPS (*dripping from the branches*). We are tears
You never wept.
We could have melted
The sharp ice-spears.
Now they fester
Deep in your breast.
The wound has closed.
Our power has gone.

PEER. Thanks. I wept in the Troll King's palace.
But I got a tail on me just the same.

BROKEN STRAWS. We are deeds
You left undone.
The strangler Doubt
Has broken and crippled us.
On the Day of Judgment
We shall be there
To tell our story.
Take care! Take care!

PEER. Dirty tricks!
Would you damn me for what I haven't done?
                    (*Hastens away.*)

AASE'S VOICE (*far away*). You're a fine driver!
  Look where you've thrown me
  Into a snowdrift!
  I'm soaking and frozen.
  You've come the wrong way!
  Oh, Peer, where's the castle?
  The Fiend's led you astray
  [With the stick from the closet].

PEER. I think I'd better be running away.
  If I have to carry the Devil's sins
  Upon my shoulders, I shan't get far.
  My own are heavy enough to bear.
                    (*Runs off.*)

Another part of the heath.

[PEER (*sings*). A gravedigger! A gravedigger! Where are
      you, dogs?
  Open your mouths and let's hear you bray!
  Let's see you girdle your hats with crepe.
  I've lots of corpses to bury today!]

(THE BUTTON MOULDER *enters from a side path with
his box of tools and a large casting-ladle.*)

BUTTON MOULDER. Well met, old man.

PEER. Good evening, friend.

BUTTON MOULDER. You're in a hurry. Where are you
      going?

PEER. To a funeral feast.

BUTTON MOULDER. Indeed? My eyes aren't too good,
      but—forgive me—
  Your name isn't by any chance Peer?

PEER. Peer Gynt, they call me.

BUTTON MOULDER. Well, that's lucky!
  You're the man I have to collect tonight.

PEER. Have to collect—? What business have you with
      me?

BUTTON MOULDER.   As you can see, I'm a button-moulder.
  You must go into my casting-ladle.

PEER.   What for?

BUTTON MOULDER.   To be melted down.

PEER.   Melted?

BUTTON MOULDER.   Yes. Look! It's clean and empty.
  Your grave is dug and your coffin is ready.
  Tonight the worms will feast in your body.
  But I have orders from my Master
  To collect your soul without delay.

PEER.   But you can't! Without warning—!

BUTTON MOULDER.   It's an ancient custom at funerals;
  As at christenings, one chooses the day,
  And the guest of honour receives no warning.

PEER.   Yes, of course. My brain's in a whirl.
  Then you are—?

BUTTON MOULDER.   I told you. A button-moulder.

PEER.   Of course.
  [One calls a favourite child by many names.]
  I see. So this is the end of my journey.
  But, my good man, this is most unfair.
  [I deserve more considerate handling than this.
  I'm not so bad as you seem to suppose.
  I've done quite a few good deeds in my life.
  At the worst I may possibly have been
  A bit of a fool.] I've never been a real sinner.

BUTTON MOULDER.   [But, my dear sir!] That is just the
    point.
  [By the highest standards you aren't a sinner.
  So] you escape the horrors of torment
  And must go with others into the casting-ladle.

PEER.   What does it matter what you call it,
  Casting-ladle or pool of fire?
  [They're the same vintage, just different bins.
  Get behind me, Satan!

BUTTON MOULDER.   You're not so rude
  As to suggest that my feet are shaped like hoofs?

PEER. Whether you've hoofs or pads or claws]
Be off with you, and take care what you do!

BUTTON MOULDER. My friend, you're labouring under a
delusion.
[We're both in a hurry, so to save time
I'll explain the gist of the matter to you.]
As you have told me with your own lips,
You aren't what one could call a whole-hearted
Sinner. You're scarcely even a minor one—

PEER. That's better. [Now you're beginning to talk sensi-
bly—]

BUTTON MOULDER. Wait a moment! You are not virtuous either—

PEER. I'm not claiming that—

BUTTON MOULDER. You're [halfway between;] neither
one nor the other.
[Nowadays one hardly ever meets a sinner
On the really grand scale.
There's more to that than just scrabbling around in the
mud.]
A man needs strength and purpose to be a sinner.

PEER. Yes, one has to be ruthless and think of nothing
else.

BUTTON MOULDER. But you weren't like that. You took
your sinning lightly.

PEER. I just splashed about on the surface.

BUTTON MOULDER. Ah, we shall soon agree. The pool of
fire
Is not for those who splash about on the surface.

PEER. And therefore, my friend, I can go as I came?

BUTTON MOULDER. No. Therefore, my friend, I must
melt you down.

[PEER. You've learned some new tricks while I've been
abroad.

BUTTON MOULDER. The custom's as old as sin. It's merely
designed
To prevent waste.] You've done it yourself.

You know that one occasionally moulds a button
That's useless. For example, without a loop.
What did you do in such a case?

PEER. Throw it away.

BUTTON MOULDER. Ah, yes. I had forgotten.
John Gynt was famous for his improvidence
[As long as he had anything in his purse].
But the Master, you see, is a thrifty man.
[That's why he's remained so prosperous.]
He never rejects as worthless anything
Which he can use again as raw material.
Now you were meant to be a shining button
On the waistcoat of the world. But your loop broke.
So you must be thrown [into the rubbish bin,
And go from there] back into the great pool.

PEER. You don't intend to melt me down with other
dead men?

BUTTON MOULDER. That is precisely what I intend.
[We've done it, you know, with quite a number of
people.
At the Royal Mint they do the same with coins
That have got so worn you can't see the face on them.

PEER. But this is the most sordid parsimony!
Oh, come on, be a sport and let me go!
A button without a loop, a worn-out shilling—
What are they to a man in your Master's position?

BUTTON MOULDER. Oh, as long as a man has some soul
left
He's always worth a little as scrap.]

PEER. No! I'll fight with all the strength I have!
Anything but this!

BUTTON MOULDER. But what else is there? Be reasonable,
now.
You're hardly qualified to go to Heaven—

PEER. [Oh, I'm not aiming as high as that.] I'm easy to
please.
[But I'm not going to give up a jot of myself.]

Give me the old-fashioned punishment.
Send me down [for a while] to serve [a sentence]
With Him with the Hoof—for a hundred years,
If need be—that's something a man can bear,
For they say the suffering's only spiritual.
And I think that ought to be fairly tolerable.
[It'll only be a transitional stage,
As the fox said when they started to skin him.30]
One will wait; then the hour of liberation
Will come, and I'll start another life,
And hope things will turn out somewhat better.
But this other business—to end one's days
As a speck of dirt in a stranger's body,
To be melted, and to be Peer Gynt no more—
It fills my soul with revulsion.

BUTTON MOULDER. But, my dear Peer, there's really no need
To get so upset. You have never been yourself.
What does it matter if you disappear?

PEER. I have never been—? I could almost laugh!
Have I ever been anything but myself?
No, button-moulder, you're guessing blindly.
If you could look into my heart
You'd find Peer Gynt and only him;
Nobody else, nothing less nor more.

BUTTON MOULDER. It's impossible. Here are my orders. Look,
It is written: "Thou shalt claim Peer Gynt.
He has defied the Master's intention;
He is waste, and must go to the casting-ladle."

PEER. [What nonsense!] He must mean somebody else.
Does it really say Peer? Not Rasmus or John?

BUTTON MOULDER. Oh, I melted them down long ago.
Now come along quietly, and don't waste my time.

PEER. No, I'm damned if I will! It'd be a fine thing
If it turned out tomorrow He meant someone else.
You'd better be careful, my good man.
[Consider the responsibility—]

BUTTON MOULDER. I have it in writing—

PEER. At least give me time!

BUTTON MOULDER. What good would that do?

PEER. I'll bring you proof
That I've been myself the whole of my life.
[And that's what we've been arguing about.]

BUTTON MOULDER. You'll prove it? How?

PEER. Witnesses and testimonials.

BUTTON MOULDER. I'm afraid the Master won't accept
them.

PEER. [Oh, surely!] He must! [However:
"Sufficient unto the Day is the Evil thereof."]
My good man, let me offer myself as security.
I'll soon be back. One is only born once;
[And one doesn't want to face oblivion.]
Do you agree?

BUTTON MOULDER. Very well. If you wish.
But remember. We meet at the next crossroads.

                    (PEER GYNT *runs away.*)

———————

Another part of the moor.

PEER (*runs in frantically*). [Time is money, as the Bible
says.]
If I only knew where those crossroads were!
They may be near; or they may be far.
[The earth is burning my feet like fire.]
A witness! A witness! Where shall I find one?
[It's almost impossible here in the forest.
What a mess the world is! A fine state of affairs
When a man has to prove what's obviously his right.]

(*An* OLD BENT MAN *plods by with a staff in his hand
and a pack on his back.*)

OLD MAN (*stops*). Spare a penny, kind sir, for a home-
less old man.

PEER. I'm sorry, I don't have any change—

OLD MAN. Prince Peer! Well, well! So we meet again!

PEER. Who are you?

OLD MAN. Don't you remember the Old Man of the Mountains?

PEER. Surely you're not—?

OLD MAN. The King of the Ronde, son.

PEER. [The King of the Ronde? Really?]
The King of the Ronde! [Answer me!]

OLD MAN. I'm afraid I've come down in the world—

PEER. Ruined?

OLD MAN. Robbed of every penny.
I tramp the roads, begging for food.

PEER. A witness!
My dear sir, men like you don't grow on trees—

OLD MAN. Your Highness has also aged since last we met.

PEER. [My dear father-in-law, the years take their toll.
But let's not waste time over private matters.
And above all, for God's sake, no family quarrels.]
I was a bit of a madcap in those days—

OLD MAN. Ah, well. Your Highness was young. [And youth will be youth.
But you did quite right to renounce your bride.
You saved yourself a lot of shame and bother.
She's turned out a bad one—

PEER. Has she?

OLD MAN. Gone completely to the dogs. Would you believe it?
She's gone off to live with that dreadful Trond.

PEER. Who is Trond?

OLD MAN. The troll of the Valfjeld.

PEER. Him? Oh, yes, I remember.
I once seduced three of his girls.

OLD MAN. My grandson's grown into a fine strong lad.
He's fathered children all over the country.
Fine kids, too—]

PEER. Dear father-in-law, [never mind all that.
    There's something else I have on my mind.]
    I've got into rather a difficult situation.
    I need a witness [or anyway a testimonial].
    Now you can help me better than anyone.
    I might even raise you the price of a drink.

OLD MAN. You mean I can be of service to Your High-
        ness?
    And would you give me a reference in return?

PEER. Gladly. I'm a little short of ready cash.
    [And have to economise as much as possible.]
    Now listen, and I'll explain. You remember that night
    When I came as a suitor to your palace—

OLD MAN. Of course I do, [Your Highness].

PEER. [Oh, stop this Highness business.] Now, look. You
        remember
    You wanted to slit my eye and distort my sight,
    And turn me from Peer Gynt into a troll?
    And how did I react? I resisted you.
    [I swore that I would stand on my own two feet.]
    I renounced my chances of love and power and glory
    Simply so that I could remain myself.
    Now I want you to testify to this in court—

OLD MAN. No, I can't do that.

PEER. What do you mean?

OLD MAN. You surely wouldn't force me to lie?
    You can't have forgotten. You put on troll breeches
    And sampled our mead—

PEER. [Yes, you tricked me into that.] But I refused
    To take the decisive step. And that's the test.
    [It's the final verse of the song that matters.]

OLD MAN. But it was the opposite of what you say.

PEER. What on earth do you mean?

OLD MAN.   You left the Ronde
    With my motto branded on your brow.

PEER. What motto?

OLD MAN. Those words that divide us.

PEER. Which words?

OLD MAN. Those words that distinguish troll from man:
"Troll, be thyself—and thyself alone!"

PEER (*recoils*). "Myself alone—!"

OLD MAN. Ever since then, with all your heart and soul,
You have lived your life by that principle.

PEER. I? Peer Gynt?

OLD MAN (*weeps*). You're so ungrateful.
You've lived like a troll, but have always kept it secret.
It has made you a successful man,
And now you turn up your nose at it.
[At me and the motto to which you owe everything.]

PEER. Myself alone—! A troll! An egoist!
[It's all absolute nonsense. I'm sure of it.

OLD MAN (*pulls out a wad of old newspapers*). I suppose
you imagine we trolls don't have newspapers?
Wait a second, and I'll show you in black and red
How the *Bloksberg Express* has been lauding you to the
skies,
And the *Heklefjelds Pictorial*, too, ever since you left
us.
Would you care to read them, Peer? You can if you
like.
There's an article here with the signature "Stallion-
Hoof,"
And another on "The Importance of Troll Nationalism,"
In which the writer emphasises the fact
That it isn't horns and a tail that make a troll,
It's the spirit that matters. The hallmark, he says, of
trolldom,
Is really *believing*: "To hell with the rest of the world!"
And he ends by quoting you as an example.

PEER. A mountain troll? I?]

OLD MAN. Most definitely.

PEER. You mean I could have stayed where I was,
Living in peace and luxury in the Ronde?

You mean all this worry and toil has been for nothing?
Peer Gynt a troll? It's nonsense! Be off with you.
[Here's a halfpenny. Buy yourself some tobacco.

OLD MAN.   Oh, dear, kind Prince Peer—!

PEER.   Let go! You're mad!
Or turning senile. Go to the workhouse!

OLD MAN.   That's what I'm looking for. But my grand-
son's children,
As I think I told you, are influential people,
And they're going round saying I only exist in legend.
They say there's nothing as nasty as an ungrateful
child,
And now I'm learning the truth of that for my sins.
It's a bit of a blow to become a myth in one's lifetime—

PEER.   You're not the only person to whom that's happened.

OLD MAN.   And we trolls don't have any Friendly Socie-
ties
Or Savings Banks or National Assistance.
Such institutions would never do in the Ronde.

PEER.   No. The motto there was: "Look after yourself!"

OLD MAN.   Oh, Your Highness mustn't disparage that
motto of ours.
Though, if you could possibly see your way to—

PEER.   My man,
You're barking up the wrong tree.] Anyway, I'm completely broke.

OLD MAN.   No! Your Highness a beggar?

PEER.   Yes. I've even had to pawn my [princely] self.
And that's your fault, you and your bloody trolls.
[It shows the danger of keeping bad company.]

OLD MAN.   Oh dear, that's another hope gone.
Well, goodbye. I'd best be moving on towards town.

PEER.   What will you do there?

OLD MAN.   Try to get on the stage.
[I hear they're advertising for local talent.]

PEER.   The best of luck! [You can give them a kiss from
me!]
If I get out of this, I'll come and join you.
[I'll write them a farce both witty and profound. I—
Yes! I think I'll call it *sic transit gloria mundi!*]
        (*He runs off down the road. The* OLD MAN
                is left shouting after him.)

————————

At a crossroads.

[PEER.   Well, my lad, you're really up against it now.
That "To hell with the rest of the world" has fairly sunk
you.
Your ship's a wreck; you must find some straw to cling
to.
Anything rather than go into the waste bin.]

BUTTON MOULDER (*at the crossroads*).   Well now, Peer.
Have you found your witnesses?

PEER.   A crossroads already? That didn't take long.

BUTTON MOULDER.   I can see from your face that you've
failed.
[Your face is a poster telling me the news.
I don't have to ask for a paper to find what's happened.]

PEER.   I got tired of the hunt. One could lose one's way—

BUTTON MOULDER.   Yes. And anyway, where does it lead?

[PEER.   True enough; in the forest, at nightfall—]

BUTTON MOULDER.   But there's an old man trudging
along.
Shall we call him?

PEER.   No, let him go. He's drunk.

BUTTON MOULDER.   But he might be able to—

PEER.   Hush! No! Let him go!

BUTTON MOULDER.   Well, shall we be off?

PEER.   One question. What does it mean: "To be oneself"?

BUTTON MOULDER. That's a strange question, from a man
Who a moment ago—

PEER. Come on, answer me!

BUTTON MOULDER. To be oneself is: to kill oneself.
But I suppose that explanation's wasted on you.
Let us say: always to serve the Master's intention.

PEER. But what of a man who never learned
What the Master intended him to be?

BUTTON MOULDER. His instinct should guide him.

PEER. But instinct can often lead you astray.
[And then you're lost before you're halfway.]

BUTTON MOULDER. Very true, Peer Gynt. And in this
bad instinct
He with the Hoof has his best angel.

PEER. [This is a damnably complicated business.]
Right. I abandon my claim of having been myself.
[It might be difficult to get proof of that.
I accept that part of my case as lost.]
But a moment ago, when I was alone on the moor,
[I felt the shoe of my conscience pinching me.]
I said to myself: "It's true. You are a sinner—"

BUTTON MOULDER. Now we're back where we started—

PEER. No, no. I mean a great sinner.
[Not merely in deed, but also in thought and word.
When I was abroad, I behaved very badly—]

BUTTON MOULDER. Maybe. I must ask you to show me
the proof—

PEER. Yes, just give me time. I'll find a priest,
Make a confession, and bring you a certificate—

BUTTON MOULDER. Yes, if you can bring me that
You will certainly avoid the casting-ladle.
But, Peer, I have my orders—

PEER. That paper's out of date. It was made out years
ago
[When I was leading a careless, lazy life,
Playing the Prophet, pretending to be a Fatalist].
Well, can I try?

BUTTON MOULDER.   But—

PEER.   Please!
   Oh, please! I'm sure you can't be all that busy.
   [The air round here is excellent for the health.
   It lengthens people's lives considerably.
   You know what the priest at Justedal[31] once said:
   "Hardly anyone ever dies in this valley."]

BUTTON MOULDER.   Till the next crossroads, then. But not
        a step further.

PEER.   I'll find a priest! If I have to drag him by his
        cassock—!

                   (*He starts running.*)

_____

A *hillside covered with heather. A path winds up towards the mountains.*

[PEER.   You never know what may turn out useful,
   As Esben said when he found the magpie's wing.[32]
   Who'd ever have guessed that a list of one's sins
   Could prove a man's salvation on his last night?
   Mind, the situation's still just as tricky.
   Would the ladle really be worse than the fire?
   Ah, well. While there's life, they say there's hope.
   That's a proverb that's stood the test of time.]

(*A* THIN PERSON, *in a priest's cassock tucked high and
with a fowling-net over his shoulder, comes running down
the path.*)

PEER.   What's this? A priest [with a fowling-net]!
   Hurrah! I'm in luck. Good evening, your Reverence.
   Awkward going, isn't it?

THIN PERSON.   Indeed. But what wouldn't one do for a
        soul?

PEER.   Oh, is someone about to go to heaven?

THIN PERSON.   I trust not.

PEER.   May I accompany your Reverence for a little of
        the way?

THIN PERSON.   With pleasure. I am fond of company.

PEER.   I should like to consult you—

THIN PERSON.   Proceed.

PEER.   I'm a good man. Always been law-abiding.
  Never been inside. But you know how it is,
  Sometimes a man puts his foot wrong and stumbles—

THIN PERSON.   Ah, yes. That happens to the best of us.

PEER.   Well, these trifles—

THIN PERSON.   Trifles?

PEER.   Yes, only trifles.
  [I've never done anything really wicked—]

THIN PERSON.   Then, my dear sir, you're wasting my time.
  I'm not the person you seem to think me.
  What are you looking at? [You find my fingers in-
     teresting?

PEER.   Your nails are somewhat strikingly developed.

THIN PERSON.   And now I see you're studying my feet.]

PEER (*points*).   Is that hoof natural?[33]

THIN PERSON.   So I flatter myself.

PEER (*raises his hat*).   I thought you were only a priest.
  And I have the honour—! Well!
  One mustn't look a gift horse in the—I mean, I'm de-
     lighted!
  [If you find the front door open, why go through the
     back?
  If the King puts his head out of the window
  You can raise your fingers at the footman.]

THIN PERSON.   Give me your hand. You seem remarkably
     unbiassed.
  Now, my dear fellow, what can I do for you?
  [Er—you mustn't ask me to give you power or money.
  I couldn't do that if you put a noose round my neck.
  You can't imagine how dead business has been
  Lately. Trade's been completely at a standstill.
  There just aren't the souls. Just the odd stray now and
     then.

PEER.   Has mankind taken a turn for the better, then?

THIN PERSON.   Quite the contrary. They've deteriorated
   disgracefully.

Most of them are only fit for the casting-ladle.

PEER.   Yes, I've heard about that ladle. Actually
That was what I wanted to talk to you about.]

THIN PERSON.   You may open your heart to me.

PEER.   If it isn't too much to ask, I'd like—

THIN PERSON.   A place of refuge? Hm?

PEER.   You've guessed [before I even opened my mouth.
You said just now that business has been bad,
So I thought you might conceivably stretch a point—

THIN PERSON.   But, my dear sir—]

PEER.   I don't ask much.
I could even manage without a salary.
Just decent treatment—as far as circumstances permit—

THIN PERSON.   A warm room?

PEER.   Not too warm.
And, if possible, [freedom to come and go
As I please; and especially] the right to return
If I get the offer of anything better.

THIN PERSON.   My dear friend, it pains me to say this, but
You can't imagine how many similar applications
I receive from people departing their earthly life.

PEER.   But think of the wicked life I've led!
[Surely I am eminently qualified for admission?]

THIN PERSON.   You said they were trifles—

PEER.   Only in a sense. But, now I remember,
I trafficked in slaves—

THIN PERSON.   There are men who have trafficked in
   hearts and souls,
[But they made a mess of the job] and failed to get in.

PEER.   I shipped heathen idols to China.

THIN PERSON.   Oh, [don't talk rubbish!] We laugh at such
   things!
[There are people who set up much nastier idols

In art and literature, and sermons for that matter;
And even they don't get in.]

PEER.   Yes, but wait a minute!
Do you know, I once pretended to be a Prophet?

THIN PERSON.   Who hasn't? [Most people's *Sehen ins
            Blaue*
Ends in the casting-ladle.] No, I'm sorry.
If you haven't any better credentials than these,
I can't let you in [however much I might like to].

PEER.   But listen! In a shipwreck
[I was clinging to an upturned boat.
There's a saying: "A drowning man will clutch at a
            straw";
But there's another: "Charity begins at home,"
And] I half robbed a poor cook of his life.

THIN PERSON.   I don't mind if you half robbed a kitchen-
            maid
Of something else. [Don't waste my time
With all this rubbish about halves. I'm sorry,]
Do you think I can waste expensive fuel
On people like you in difficult times like these?
[Now, don't get angry. It's only your sins
That I'm disparaging. I'm sure you'll forgive me
For speaking out so straight. So, my dear fellow,]
Put these ideas out of your head.
Resign yourself to the casting-ladle. What good
Would it be to you if I offered you board and lodging?
Think a minute. You're a sensible man.
You'd keep your memory, that's true enough,
But what have you got to remember?
I promise you, the memory of things past
Would give you little joy.
You'd find no cause for weeping or for laughter,
No cause for rejoicing or despair,
Nothing to fire your heart, or freeze your blood;
They'd merely be a source of irritation.

PEER.   You may be right. [It isn't easy to know
Where the shoe pinches when one hasn't got it on.]

THIN PERSON.   [That's true. I myself, thanks to Never
    Mind Whom,
Only need one shoe. Incidentally,
It's lucky that you happened to mention shoes.
That reminds me] I must be on my way.
I've a joint to collect; a nice, juicy roast.
[So I can't waste time exchanging pleasantries here.]

PEER.   If one may ask, what sins made him grow fat?

THIN PERSON.   I understand that all his life
He has been himself. [Which of course qualifies him.]

PEER.   Himself? You mean such people
Are automatically your parishioners?

THIN PERSON.   That depends. [The door is—left ajar.]
There are two ways in which a man can be himself.
A right way and a wrong way.
You may know that a man in Paris
Has discovered a way of taking portraits
With the help of the sun. Either one can produce
A direct picture, or else what they call a negative.
In the latter, light and dark are reversed;
And the result, to the ordinary eye, is ugly.
But the image of the original is there.
All that's required is to develop it.
Now if a human soul, in the course of its life,
Has created one of these negative portraits,
The plate is not destroyed. They send it to me.
[I give it treatment, and by suitable means
Effect a metamorphosis.] I develop it.
I steam it and dip it, I burn it and cleanse it
With sulphur and similar ingredients,
Till the picture appears which the plate was intended to
    give.
[I mean, the one known as the positive.]
But when a soul like you has smudged himself out,
Even sulphur and potash can achieve nothing.

PEER.   Then one must come to you as black as a raven
To be sent back as white as a dove? May I ask what
    name

Is scratched beneath this particular negative
[Which you are about to burn into a positive]?

THIN PERSON. The name is Peter Gynt.

PEER. Peter Gynt? Indeed? Is Mr. Gynt himself?

THIN PERSON. So he affirms.

PEER. Well, he's a reliable man.

THIN PERSON. You know him?

PEER. In a way.

[You know how it is. One knows so many people.]

THIN PERSON. [My time is short.] Where did you see him
  last?

PEER. Down at the Cape.

THIN PERSON. Of Good Hope?

PEER. Yes, but I understand he's leaving very soon.

THIN PERSON. Then I must be off at once. I hope I'm in
  time
  To catch him. I never liked that Cape of Good Hope.
  It's always full of missionaries from Stavanger.
                                  (*Runs off southwards.*)

PEER. The silly bastard! Look at him,
  Running away with his tongue hanging out!
  Well, I made a fool out of him.
  [Putting on airs and acting big!]
  A fat lot he's got to boast about!
  [He won't get rich the way he's going.]
  He'll be knocked off his perch. [And his whole show
    with him.]
  Hm. I'm not too safe myself.
  I've been expelled from the privileged circle;
  The exclusive club of men who are themselves.
                  (*A shooting star is seen. He nods after it.*)
  Hail, brother star! A greeting from Peer Gynt!
  We flash for a moment, then our light is quenched,
  And we disappear into the void for ever.
  (*He composes himself as though frightened, and goes
  deeper into the mist. There is silence for a few moments,
  then he cries:*)

Is there no one, no one in all the Universe—
No one in the Abyss—no one in Heaven—!

(*He comes forward again further down, throws his hat down on the road, and tears his hair. Gradually a calmness comes over him.*)

How unspeakably poor a soul can be
When it enters the mist and returns to nothing!
O beautiful earth, don't be angry with me
That I trod your sweet grass to no avail.
O beautiful sun, you have squandered
Your golden light upon an empty hut.
There was no one within to warm and comfort.
The owner, I know now, was never at home.
Beautiful sun and beautiful earth,
Why did you bear my mother and give her light?
The spirit is mean, and Nature is wasteful.
Life is a terrible price to pay for birth.
I want to climb, up to the highest peak.
I want to see the sun rise once again,
To gaze till I am tired at the promised land.
Then let the snow pile over me,
And let them write above: "Here lies no one."
And afterwards—let the world take its course.

CHURCHGOERS (*singing on the forest path*).   O thrice blest
    morn, when tongues of fire
God's spirit did proclaim!
O Holy Ghost, our souls inspire
To sing in universal choir,
And praise God's glorious name!

PEER (*crouches in terror*).   Never look there! That's waste
    and desert!
I was a dead man long before I died!
      (*He tries to slink in among the bushes,
        but comes upon the crossroads.*)

BUTTON MOULDER.   Good morning. Where is your list of
    sins?

PEER.   I've shouted and whistled all over the heath.

BUTTON MOULDER.   And met no one?

PEER.   Only a [travelling] photographer.

BUTTON MOULDER.   Well, your time is up.

PEER.   Yes. Everything's up.
  The owl smells the light. Can you hear him hooting?

BUTTON MOULDER.   It's the mattins bell.

PEER (*points*).   What's that shining over there?

BUTTON MOULDER.   Only light from a hut.

PEER.   What is that sound I hear like sighing?

BUTTON MOULDER.   A woman singing.

PEER.   There! Yes! There I'll find my sins!

BUTTON MOULDER (*grips him*).   Set thy house in order!
      (*They have come out of the undergrowth and
      are standing by the cabin. Day breaks.*)

PEER.   My house? It's there! Away! Begone!
  If your ladle were as large as a coffin
  It would be too small for me and my sins.

BUTTON MOULDER.   Well, the third crossroads, Peer. But
      then—!
              (*Turns aside, and goes.*)

PEER (*approaches the cabin*).   Forward or back it's
      equally far.
  Outside or in, I'm still confined.
              (*Stops.*)
  No! I hear like a wild, unending cry:
  "Go in! Go back! Go home!"
          (*Goes a few steps, then stops again.*)
  "Go round," said the Boyg.
          (*Hears the song from inside the cabin.*)
  "Ah! No! This time straight through,
  However narrow the path may be."
(*He runs towards the cabin. At the same moment,*
SOLVEIG *appears in the doorway, dressed for church, with
a psalmbook wrapped in linen and a staff in her hand. She
stands there, erect and gentle.*)

PEER (*throws himself down on the threshold*).   Judge
      this sinner! O, speak!

SOLVEIG.   It is he! It is he! Oh, praise be to God!
    (*She gropes for him.*)

PEER.   Cry out my sins!

SOLVEIG.   You have sinned in nothing, my only child.
    (*Gropes for him again, and finds him.*)

BUTTON MOULDER (*behind the house*).   The list, Peer
  Gynt?

PEER.   Cry out my guilt!

SOLVEIG (*sits down beside him*).   You have made my life
  into a song.
Bless you for coming back to me at last.
Blessed, oh, blessed be our meeting
On this morning of Pentecost!

PEER.   Then I am lost!

SOLVEIG.   There is One Who rules all.

PEER (*laughs*).   Lost! Unless you can solve riddles.

SOLVEIG.   Tell me.

PEER.   Tell you? Yes, I will!
Can you tell me where Peer Gynt has been
[Since you saw him last]?

SOLVEIG.   Been?

PEER.   With the mark of destiny on his brow
As he sprang forth in the mind of God!
Can you answer me that? If not, I must go
To my home, down to the land of mists.

SOLVEIG (*smiles*).   Oh, that riddle is easy.

PEER.   Tell me, then!
Where was my self, my whole self, my true self?
The self that bore God's stamp upon its brow?

SOLVEIG.   In my faith, in my hope, and in my love.

PEER (*starts back*).   What do you say? Hush! Now you
  speak in riddles!
Ah! *You* are the mother to that child?

SOLVEIG.   Yes, I am. But who is its father?
It is He Who forgives when the mother prays.

PEER (*bathed in light, cries*). My mother! My wife! O,
  thou pure woman!
  O hide me in your love! Hide me! Hide me!
    (*He clings tightly to her and buries his face in
    her lap. A long silence. The sun rises.*)

SOLVEIG (*sings softly*). Sleep, O sleep, my dearest boy.
  I will cradle you, I will guard you.
  Sleep, O sleep, my love, my joy.
  Sleep now, and rest.

  You've sat on my lap, we've played together.
  The life-long day you've lain on my breast.
  You've always been close to my heart
  Now you're tired. You can rest.
                    (*Hums*)
  Sleep, O sleep—

BUTTON MOULDER'S VOICE (*behind the house*). We shall
  meet at the last crossroads, Peer.
  [And then we'll see if—! I'll say no more.]

SOLVEIG (*sings louder as the daylight grows*). I will cradle you, I will guard you.
  Sleep, sleep and dream.

NOTES

1. *Changeling.* There is an old Norwegian superstition that changelings left by the fairies can be blown up the chimney.

2. *Master Cook.* A kind of master of ceremonies.

3. *Saeter.* A small mountain farm where the cattle are sent to pasture in summer.

4. *Troll, be thyself—and thyself alone!* The phrase which Ibsen uses to formulate the philosophy of the trolls, *at vaere sig selv nok*, to be self-sufficient in a bad sense, was not, as many critics have assumed, created by Ibsen. The danger of self-sufficiency was a problem which was occupying people during the middle of the nineteenth century far outside the boundaries of Norway. Professor Gunnar Tideström has pointed out (in an article in the Swedish magazine *Prisma* in January 1950) that English writers around this time were debating the reasons why the word self-sufficiency had acquired a pejorative significance; De Quincey suggested that *self-sufficingness* should be used to convey the original nobility of the Greek *autarkes* and the Latin *sibi sufficiens;* and Swinburne proposed *self-sufficience* as an alternative in, curiously enough, 1867, the very year in which Ibsen wrote *Peer Gynt*. The absence in modern English of any pejorative equivalent of self-sufficiency makes this vital phrase peculiarly difficult to translate. The usual: "Troll, to thyself be enough" fails for this reason, apart from being deficient in any real impact. There is an almost exact equivalent of *at vaere sig selv nok* in the modern slang expression: "I'm all right, Jack!"; but one can hardly put this into the mouth of a nineteenth-century troll. In the final scene with the Old

Man (pp. 145–46), where the word *nok* is used repeatedly by itself, I have used two variant translations, "Look after yourself" and "To hell with the rest of the world", in an attempt to clarify the meaning; no single English phrase quite suffices.

5. *Salted herring*. The traditional remedy in Scandinavia for a hangover.

6. *Why, he's chopped his finger off!* This episode is based on a true incident of which Ibsen had read in the newspaper *Aftenbladet* on June 14, 1864. He had already used it in the epic version of *Brand*, of which he completed a considerable portion before abandoning it to treat the subject as a play. But there the boy had been a figure of shame; in *Peer Gynt* he appears as a man of honour, who had the courage to do what other men secretly wished to do. It is difficult not to believe that Ibsen's preoccupation with this matter stemmed from the sense of guilt which we know he possessed for not having taken part in the Danish-German war, about which he felt so strongly.

The lines describing this incident were cut in production because the audience was able to see it silently taking place.

7. *Soria-Moria*. The Arabic name for a group of islands beyond the Red Sea which were fabled to be the Islands of the Blest.

8. *Grane*. Sigurd Fafnirsbane's horse, descended from the god Odin's Sleipnir.

9. *Trumpeterstraale*. In the original, Herr Trumpeterstraale is a Swede, but since some of his remarks, about Charles XII's spurs and so forth, have no meaning for an English audience, we turned him, in the Old Vic production, into an American. This involved the alteration of a single line on page 75 (see footnote 13 below).

10. *A measure of spiritual contemplation . . .* This speech is deliberately obscure in the original, as a satire on the German tendency to talk abstract nonsense.

11. *Lippe-Detmold*. A tiny German principality.

12. *Your Reich last for a thousand years!* Literally: "Our finest and most ancient Rhenish vintages!"

13. *Stand in history with Charlemagne!* Literally: "And all the swords of Charles XII!"

14. *King Charles's spurs.* When King Charles XII of Sweden was fighting the Turks at Bender (in Bessarabia, on the Dniester) in 1713, his spurs are said to have tripped him and resulted in his capture. There is also a legend that he tore with these spurs the garments of the Turkish emissary who brought him the news that the Sultan had concluded a truce with their mutual enemy Peter the Great of Russia.

15. *But under protest.* This is probably a gibe at Count Manderström, the Swedish Foreign Minister who, when Germany had attacked Denmark in 1864, had written diplomatic notes of protest but had refrained from taking any positive action. Manderström is also supposed to have been the original of the minister Hussein in the madhouse scene (see page 111). Ibsen had a particular contempt for him, and once drew a halter round his neck on a picture of him in an illustrated magazine in the Scandinavian Club in Rome. Manderström's nephew, Carl Snoilsky, later became one of Ibsen's closest friends.

16. *Gyntiana.* Ole Bull, Ibsen's old chief at the Bergen Theatre, had tried in 1852 to found an ideal Norwegian colony in Pennsylvania, on the model approved by the French Socialists. He called it Oleana; but it ended in financial disaster.

17. *Kaba.* A sacred building in Mecca, containing a black stone which pilgrims have to kiss.

18. *Das ewig weibliche ziehet uns an!* A deliberate misquotation of the last line of Goethe's *Faust*. Goethe's line reads: "Woman eternally draws us upwards." Peer says: "Woman eternally draws us towards her."

19. *Qu'allais-je faire dans cette galère?* A quotation, slightly wrong as always with Peer, from Molière's comedy, *Les Fourberies de Scapin:* "What the devil was I doing in that boat?" Peer has already used this once, on page

87, where I have translated it: "Why did I ever get on to that waggon?"

20. *Becker*. Becker's *Weltgeschichte* (1801–9) had been translated into Danish in the middle of the nineteenth century.

21. *Memnon*. Memnon was the god of the morning. When he died, his mother Aurora begged Jupiter to honour him. Jupiter answered her prayer by turning Memnon's ashes into birds that perpetually sang, fought and played. These lines are not, as has often been supposed, meaningless, nor does their significance seem to me obscure. The statue is telling Peer that the latter has sealed up his soul, and that unless he can unseal it he will die— as indeed he does. Whether Peer dies in the madhouse, or in the shipwreck, the last scenes of the play surely show us either his soul's passage through purgatory, or the film of his life, with its failures and errors, unreeling before his eyes in the moment of death. It is interesting to note that Ibsen had written of the Memnon Statue as early as 1855, in a prologue spoken from the stage at the Bergen Theatre.

22. *The Circle of the Seventy Interpreters*. Presumably a reference to the writers of the Septuagint, the Greek version of the Old Testament said to have been made by seventy translators around 270 B.C. Various unlikely suggestions have been put forward as to the meaning of Begriffenfeldt's next sentence, "recently increased to a hundred and sixty," but I think this is probably merely intended as an additional example of the German's lunacy.

23. *Munchausen's fox*. Baron Munchausen claimed to have nailed a fox to a tree by its tail, cut a slit in its forehead, and whipped it so that it jumped out of its skin.

24. *Huhu*. This character is a caricature of the Norwegian *maalstraevere*, "a party," to quote William Archer, "which desired to substitute a language compounded of the various local dialects for the Norwegian of the bourgeoisie and of literature, which they called Danish, and declared to be practically a foreign tongue to the peasants and lower classes generally. The peasants, they argued,

(like Ibsen's orang-outangs) lived and died 'uninter-
preted.' The movement attained no little force in the
[eighteen-]sixties and seventies, and a considerable literature sprang up in the so-called *maal*, the work of such men
as Ivar Aasen, A. O. Vinje, and Kristofer Janson." Janson
was furious when he read this scene and wrote a virulent
attack on the play in *Aftenbladet*, expressing the hope
that Ibsen would soon "tire of spitting and scolding from
his chimney corner."

25. *Fellah*. A fellah is an Egyptian peasant. This character with the mummy on his back is an expression of a
theme frequently to be found in Ibsen's work, especially of
this period: man's bondage to his past. A few years later
he was to write a poem on this theme entitled *The Corpse
in the Cargo*; and it is, of course, the central *motif* of
Ghosts. The Dovre kingdom and Aase's ruined farm are
parallel symbols; but they should not be taken, as they
have been, as referring specifically to Norway's, or Sweden's, glorification of her former greatness. The image of
the Fellah and his mummy may have been based on the
adulation shown by the Swedes towards the mummified
body of Charles XII, and there are references in the troll
scene which are aimed at Norwegian chauvinism; but it
was humanity's bondage, not Norway's, that troubled Ibsen
most deeply.

26. *Cuckold to Death and to Aslak the smith*. Because
Aslak and, now, Death have both slept with Ingrid since
Peer seduced her on her wedding night; she is another
person who has been destroyed by his greed. The Man in
Grey is, of course, Mads Moen.

27. *The Cat of the Dovre*. The white bear which Peer
Gynt took with him (in Asbjoernsen's tale) to frighten
the trolls on Christmas Eve.

28. *I think I'll put up my own rubbish for auction*. The
word auction had painful associations for Ibsen. In a letter
to Bjoernson (undated, but probably written in October
1866, just before he started *Peer Gynt*), he expressed
vehement indignation at the fact that his belongings in

Norway had been auctioned without his authorisation. "It isn't so much the loss of my furniture, etc., that grieves me, but that my private letters, papers, drafts etc., not to speak of many things that meant far more to me than their face value, should have found their way into the hands of any Tom, Dick or Harry, is a most bitter thought."

29. *Threadballs*. Trolls in threadballs are a common idea in Norwegian folk lore.

30. *It'll only be a transitional stage, As the fox said when they started to skin him*. A reference to the Norwegian proverb: " 'It'll be a change,' as the fox said when they started to skin him."

31. *Justedal*. Matthias Foss, a priest in Justedal in the middle of the eighteenth century, wrote in 1750 "A Short Description of Justedal," which included the sentence: "They [i.e., the people of Justedal] are exceedingly long-lived, so that it is seldom anyone dies there."

32. *Esben*. Esben Askeladd is a character in a Norwegian folk tale who found a dead magpie which led to his winning the hand of a princess.

33. *Is that hoof natural?* The Devil is traditionally represented in Scandinavian folk lore as having a single hoof instead of a right foot.

ACKNOWLEDGMENTS

I gladly express my thanks to Michael Elliott for many valuable suggestions concerning the translation; also to the Old Vic Theatre Company for commissioning it, and to everyone concerned with that memorable production.

I also gratefully acknowledge my debt to the writings of Professor Francis Bull, the greatest of Ibsen scholars, particularly to his monograph on the play (Oslo, 1956) and his introduction in the centenary edition of Ibsen's works (Volume VI, Oslo, 1931).

Permission to quote from Ibsen's letters has been kindly granted by Gyldendal Norsk Forlag of Oslo, Norway.

M. M.

ANCHOR BOOKS

DRAMA

THE ANCHOR ANTHOLOGY OF JACOBEAN DRAMA, Vol. II—Richard C. Harrier, ed., AC5b

AN ANTHOLOGY OF GERMAN EXPRESSIONIST DRAMA: A Prelude to the Absurd. Rubiner, *Man in the Center*; Kornfeld, *Epilogue to the Actor*; Goll, *Two Superdramas* and *The Immortal One*; Kaiser, *Man in the Tunnel* and *Alkiblades Saved*; Kokoschka, *Murderer the Woman's Hope* and *Job*; Sorge, *The Beggar*; Sternheim, *The Strong Box*; Hasenclever, *Humanity*; Lauckner, *Cry in the Street*; Brecht, *Baal*—Walter A. Sokol, ed., A365

AN APPROACH TO SHAKESPEARE—D. A. Traversi, A74

BRAND—Henrik Ibsen, Michael Meyer, trans., A215a

BRECHT: THE MAN AND HIS WORK—Martin Esslin, A245

THE CLASSIC THEATRE, Vol. I: Six Italian Plays. Machiavelli, *The Mandrake*; Beolio, *Ruzzante Returns from the Wars*; Goldini, *The Servant of Two Masters* and *Mirandolina*; Gozzi, *The King Stag*; (Anon), *The Three Cuckolds*—Eric Bentley, ed., A155a

THE CLASSIC THEATRE, Vol. II: Five German Plays. Goethe, *Egmont*; Schiller, *Don Carlos* and *Mary Stuart*; Kleist, *Penthesilea* and *The Prince of Homburg*—Eric Bentley, ed., A155b

THE CLASSIC THEATRE, Vol. III: Six Spanish Plays. Fernando de Rojas, *Celestina*; Cervantes, *The Siege of Jumantia*; Lope, *Fuente Ovejuna*; Tirso, *The Trickster of Seville*; Calderon, *Love After Death* and *Life is a Dream*—Eric Bentley, ed., A155c

THE CLASSIC THEATRE, Vol. IV: Six French Plays. Corneille, *The Cid*; Molière, *The Misanthrope*; Racine, *Phaedra*; Lesage, *Turcaret*; Marivaux, *The False Confession*; Beaumarchais, *Figaro's Marriage*—Eric Bentley, ed., A155d

COMEDY—Henri Bergson and George Meredith, A87

THE COMPLETE PLAYS OF WILLIAM WYCHERLEY—ed. by Gerald Weales, AC8

Drama (continued)

FIVE COMEDIES OF ARISTOPHANES, A57

FIVE PLAYS OF STRINDBERG—Elizabeth Sprigge, trans., A219

GHOSTS AND THREE OTHER PLAYS: A Doll's House; An Enemy of the People; Rosmersholm—Henrik Ibsen; trans. by Michael Meyer, A215e

GOETHE'S FAUST with the original German on facing pages—Walter Kaufmann, trans., A328

GREEK TRAGEDY—H. D. F. Kitto, A38

HAMLET AND OEDIPUS—Ernest Jones, A31

HEDDA GABLER AND THREE OTHER PLAYS—Henrik Ibsen, Michael Meyer, trans., A215c

THE HUMAN IMAGE IN DRAMATIC LITERATURE—Francis Fergusson, A124

THE IDEA OF A THEATER—Francis Fergusson, A4

THE IMMEDIATE EXPERIENCE—Robert Warshow, A410

INFERNO, ALONE and Other Writings—August Strindberg, trans. by Evert Sprinchorn, A492c

MADMAN'S DEFENSE—August Strindberg, trans. by Evert Sprinchorn, A492b

THE MODERN THEATRE, Vol. I: Buchner, Woyzeck; Verga, Cavalleria Rusticana; Becque, Woman of Paris; Brecht, The Three Penny Opera; Giraudoux, Electra—Eric Bentley, ed., A48a

THE MODERN THEATRE, Vol. II: Musset, Fantasio; Ostrovsky, The Diary of a Scoundrel; Schnitzler, La Ronde; Yeats, Purgatory; Brecht, Mother Courage—Eric Bentley, ed., A48b

THE MODERN THEATRE, Vol. III: Gogol, Gamblers; Labiche and Marc-Michel, An Italian Straw Hat; Conrad, One More Day; Giraudoux, Judith; Anouilh, Thieves' Carnival—Eric Bentley, ed., A48c

THE MODERN THEATRE, Vol. IV: From the American Drama—Swerling, Burrows, & Loesser, Guys and Dolls; Fitch, Captain Jinks of the Horse Marines; Mitchell, The New York Idea; Wilder, Pullman Car Hiawatha; Saroyan, The Man with the Heart in the Highlands—Eric Bentley, ed., A48d

THE MODERN THEATRE, Vol. V: Buchner, Danton's Death; Gogol, The Marriage; Ghelderode, Escurial; Anouilh, Medea; O'Casey, Cock-a-Doodle Dandy—Eric Bentley, ed., A48e

THE MODERN THEATRE, Vol. VI: Musset, Lorenzaccio; Wedekind, Spring's Awakening; Sternheim, The Underpants; Beerbohm, A Social Success; Brecht, The Measures Taken—Eric Bentley, ed., A48f

PEER GYNT—Henrik Ibsen, Michael Meyer, trans., A215d

SHAKESPEARE—Mark Van Doren, A11

SHAKESPEARE OUR CONTEMPORARY—Jan Kott, trans. by Boleslaw Taborski, A499

SIX PLAYS OF PLAUTUS—Lionel Casson, trans., A367

SIX PLAYS OF STRINDBERG—Elizabeth Sprigge, trans., A54

THE SON OF A SERVANT: The Story of the Evolution of a Human Being (1849–1867)—August Strindberg, trans. by Evert Sprinchorn, A492a

SOPHOCLES' OEDIPUS THE KING AND OEDIPUS AT COLONUS—A New Translation for Modern Audiences and Readers by Charles R. Walker, A496

STUDIES IN SEVENTEENTH-CENTURY FRENCH LITERATURE—Jean-Jacques Demorest, ed., A503

THEATRE OF THE ABSURD—Martin Esslin, A279

THEORIES OF COMEDY—Paul Lauter, ed., A403

TUDOR PLAYS: An Anthology of Early English Drama—ed. by Edmund Creeth, AO-1

WHEN WE DEAD AWAKEN AND THREE OTHER PLAYS—Henrik Ibsen, Michael Meyer, trans., A215b

MUSIC

BEETHOVEN'S LETTERS, JOURNALS AND CONVERSATIONS—Michael Hamburger, ed., A206

BRAHMS: HIS LIFE AND WORK—Karl Geiringer, A248

COMPOSER'S WORLD—Paul Hindemith, A235

DARWIN, MARX, WAGNER—Jacques Barzun, A127

AN ELIZABETHAN SONGBOOK—Noah Greenberg, W. H. Auden and Chester Kallman, A56

PUCCINI LIBRETTOS—In New English Translations by William Weaver with the Original Italian, A531

RING OF WORDS: An Anthology of Song Texts—ed. and trans. by Philip L. Miller, A428

VERDI LIBRETTOS—William Weaver, trans., A342